Spanish Gardens and Patios

Mildred Stapley Byne
& Arthur Byne

CORRESPONDING MEMBERS OF THE HISPANIC SOCIETY OF AMERICA; AUTHORS OF "SPANISH IRONWORK," "SPANISH ARCHITECTURE OF THE XVI CENTURY," "SPANISH INTERIORS AND FURNITURE," ETC.

4880 Lower Valley Road, Atglen, PA 19310 USA

Library of Congress Control Number: 2007938034

Designed by "Sue"

ISBN: 978-0-7643-2834-3
Printed in China

Schiffer Books are available at special discounts for bulk purchases for sales promotions or premiums. Special editions, including personalized covers, corporate imprints, and excerpts can be created in large quantities for special needs. For more information contact the publisher:

Published by Schiffer Publishing Ltd.
4880 Lower Valley Road
Atglen, PA 19310
Phone: (610) 593-1777; Fax: (610) 593-2002
E-mail: Info@schifferbooks.com

For the largest selection of fine reference books on this and related subjects, please visit our web site at www.schifferbooks.com
We are always looking for people to write books on new and related subjects. If you have an idea for a book please contact us at the above address.

This book may be purchased from the publisher.
Include $3.95 for shipping.
Please try your bookstore first.
You may write for a free catalog.

In Europe, Schiffer books are distributed by
Bushwood Books
6 Marksbury Ave.
Kew Gardens
Surrey TW9 4JF England
Phone: 44 (0) 20 8392-8585; Fax: 44 (0) 20 8392-9876
E-mail: info@bushwoodbooks.co.uk
Website: www.bushwoodbooks.co.uk
Free postage in the U.K., Europe; air mail at cost.

PREFACE

Interest in Spanish design dates back to the founding of the New World, and has peaked in many waves. Leaders of one such wave in the early part of the 20th Century were the husband and wife team of Mildred Stapley Byne (1875-1941) and Arthur Byne. They were passionate purveyors of all things Spanish, authoring many books on the subject of Spain and Spanish style, and working as active members of the Hispanic Society of America.

Mildred did much of the writing, Arthur the photography, and together they left a wonderful legacy. Their publications include works published with the Hispanic Society, like the lavishly illustrated *Spanish Ironwork* published in 1915.

Mildred even promoted Spanish history and culture with books like a biography of Christopher Columbus, and articles for magazines such as Harper's, including "The Great Queen Isabella," June 1912 and the "City of Towers," October 1911.

This book is one of many they published that document Spanish influence on architecture and landscaping. Their other works included three volumes of *Spanish Interiors and Furniture: Photographs, Drawings and Text* published between 1922 and 1925. Their work could be quite detailed and studious, as in the 1917 *Spanish Architecture of the Sixteenth Century* and the 1920 volume entitled *Decorated Wooden Ceilings in Spain*.

Other published work included Sculptured Capital in Spain: A Series of Examples Dating from the Sixth to the Sixteenth Century and an illustrated travel log entitled Forgotten Shrines of Spain in which they explored the 1) monastery of St. Domingo de Silos, Old Castile; 2) monastery of San Zoil de Carrion de los Condes, Old Castile; 3) Royal Monastery of St. Maria del Paular, New Castile; 4) monastery of Nuestra Senora de Guadalupe, Estremadura; 5) convent of St. Clara de Moguer, Andalusia; 6) monastery of St. Maria de la Rabida, Andalusia; 7) the royal convent of Sigena, Arago; 8) and the royal monastery of St. Maria de Poblet, California.

GARDEN VISTA, CASA DEL REY MORO, RONDA
Now the villa of the Duquesa de Parcent

TO THOSE SPANIARDS WHO KINDLY OPENED THEIR GARDENS FOR STUDY AND SKETCHING, THE AUTHORS WISH TO EXPRESS THEIR GRATITUDE

FOREWORD

FOREWORD

IN PRESENTING this account of Spanish gardens it is hoped that their unusual features may attract in a practical way those who ought to have a large community of interest with the country that first carried civilization and culture to the New World.

The true Spanish garden is of Asiatic derivation; it harks back to Persia during her splendour under the Sassanids—the garden the Arabs found there when they conquered her. The Moors who made gardens in Spain, after it too had been added to the Mohammedan conquests, were no artless children of nature; their Moslem tradition was one of order, science, everything prearranged. A garden was not a walled-off piece of cultivated ground; it was a man-made design that permitted nature to play a small part, nothing more. It was a fundamentally artificial production, emphasis being laid on man's, not on nature's contribution.

And man's chief contribution was glazed polychrome tiles. These even more than the scant use of flowers make the Spanish garden unlike others of Europe. They are above all else the legacy that the Arabs and Moors left in the architecture of the Iberian Peninsula. Let no one dream of possessing a Spanish garden or patio who is hostile to their use on a generous scale.

Nor must the old-fashioned lover of flowers—our proper English heritage—expect to reconcile this with the Spanish design. It is of green he must think, especially of odorous green, and look to tiles, not to bloom, for his colour note. This briefly is the theory of the Spanish garden.

If Southern Spain receives all our attention in these chapters, it is because elsewhere in Spain gardens follow the general European tradition and so are not distinctive or to be accounted as truly Spanish gardens.

In this subject, as in all phases of Spanish art, we have on the one hand the influence of Europe and Christians, on the other, of Asia and Mohammedans. Arab civilization dominated in the south from the opening of the eighth century to the close of the fifteenth. When the Christians reconquered Cordova and Seville (1236 and 1248), and Granada (1492), they kept the Moorish artisan class and thus preserved the firmly implanted oriental tradition in the industrial arts. Domestic architecture and gardens, both so admirably adapted to the Andalusian climate, were modified slightly but not changed. The cool white house with its open patio, the small garden made for the master's delectation and not for the entertainment of his friends, were admirably suited to the reserved and exclusive character of the incoming Spaniards.

Patios are included because, being at the same time an indoor garden and an outdoor salon, they illustrate the Moorish intent to draw outdoors indoors—to have no sharp contrast between these two settings of the daily life. The only garden of dwellers in cities, it puts our small city yards to shame. "The patio," wrote Theophile Gautier, who made its acquaintance in 1840, "is a delightful invention." In truth it is much more; it is a very practical solution for house planning and a unit that offers great decorative possibilities.

A few old Andalusian cloisters are given because they represent the sort of arcade and court that served as prototype for the early missions built by Spanish priests and monks in America. The monastery having always been and still being a very prominent factor in Spanish life, it is no exaggeration to say that without the cloister no collection of Spanish gardens and patios would be complete.

A word as to the illustrations offered. Graphically a book on any phase of Spanish art, except painting, must be inadequate unless the author be prepared to act as photographer and draughtsman as well. Outside of Catalonia no group of investigators has appointed a competent photographer to record the artistic wealth of its region and *to put such photographs within reach of students*. If great architectural monuments have not received this merited attention, how much less have old gardens. The only exception to this general observation would be the perfectly obvious views sold to tourists in Seville and Granada.

This neglect of graphic record has always existed. In presenting Spanish gardens it would be a pleasure to show, as might a garden book dealing with any other country, some charming old plates engraved in the eighteenth century; but, unfortunately, Spanish archives yield no such material. When the art of engraving was at its height, Spaniards, from whom much might have been expected, made no effort to contribute. At a time when Falda, Silvestre, Scherm, Rigaud, Sutton Nichols, to mention only a few of the most important in their class, were making magnificent plates of the great gardens of Italy, France, The Lowlands, and England, nothing was produced in Spain but a few engravings of the Escorial and La Granja. True that in Andalusia many of the best Moorish gardens disappeared along with much else that was oriental soon after the Christian conquest; yet as late as the seventeenth and eighteenth centuries there still existed sufficient to repay the limner had he been interested. In the Netherlands, for instance, we read that it was the ambition of every one who owned a fine garden to have it engraved. In Spain only royalty, and very occasionally at that, shared this ambition. Indeed, even in the case of a royal and important garden like that of the Alcazar at Seville no sketch or plan can be encountered in the Castle's archives.

Our illustrations therefore—photographs, sketches, and plans—had to be made first-hand. In place of the charm of old engravings we can offer only modern accuracy and applicability.

Nor can a bibliography be offered to those who might like to pursue the subject further; until now nothing more than slight sketchy chapters here and there has been written. Certain books of horticultural and geoponic nature prepared by Spanish Arabs have been translated, but these, with one remarkable exception, are literary curiosities rather than practical helps. The exception referred to is by the Arab author Abuzacaría, whose work has just been translated by the distinguished Arabist Don José A. Sánchez Pérez. Abuzacaría, who lived in the middle of the twelfth century, had extensive farms and gardens in Aljarafe, Sevilla. He wrote all his personal observations and experiments, beside making a résumé of all the agronomic science known up to his time. For the Mohammedan world his book was law in agricultural matters. An earlier Spanish translation was made (1802), and a French (1864), but copies are now so rare as to be beyond price.

Paseo de la Castellana 19
MADRID

MARBLE TROUGH, PALACE OF THE MARQUES DE PENAFLOR
ECIJA

CONTENTS

LIST OF ILLUSTRATIONS

COLOUR-PLATES

HALF-TONES

LINE-CUTS

PART I

ANDALUSIA

I

CHARACTERISTICS AND TYPES OF SPANISH GARDENS

CHAPTER I

CHARACTERISTICS AND TYPES OF SPANISH GARDENS

NUMEROUS and beautiful must have been the gardens of Andalusia during the Mohammedan régime. To quote but one contemporary, Eben Said, a Moor of Granada who traveled through southern Spain and northern Africa in the thirteenth century: "The splendour of Andalusia appears to have spread to Tunis, where the Sultan is constructing palaces and planting gardens in our manner. All his architects are natives of Andalusia, likewise his gardeners." Small wonder that the Sultan should have summoned garden experts from Spain, for the treatise written a century before by the Sevillian Moor, Abuzacaría, with its two chapters devoted to ornamental shrubs and plants for the garden, was still the agrarian Bible of Tunis, Turkey, Egypt, Arabia, and Syria.

But in that same century, when Tunis was learning from Andalusia, the gardens whose fame had spread so far fell to new owners. Not only gardens, but all agriculture, was neglected. The Christians let the extensive and very scientific irrigation system of the Moors fall into disuse, and Southern Spain became, by comparison with its former flourishing state, a waste. To-day, the only Moorish sites still dedicated to gardens are the Alcazar (The Castle) in Seville and the Generalife in Granada. These, in spite of alterations and long periods of abandonment, preserve much of their original character. In addition, there are several simpler untouched spots like the *Patio de los Naranjos* (orange trees) in Cordova and another of similar name in Seville, both having been the gardens of the principal mosques, and, therefore, the counterpart of the Christian cloister.

When the Spaniards who domiciled themselves in the south emerged, as did other Europeans, from feudal insecurity and began to build themselves palaces and gardens, these were constructed by Moorish artisans and specialists. Naturally such works followed Moorish tradition but were modified slightly to suit the new masters. For this reason the few *early* Spanish gardens we are able to present are probably more sympathetic to European taste than would be the genuinely oriental, could the latter be found. Dating from this period, the gardens of the *Casa de las Rejas de Don Gomez* in Cordova and of the *Pilatos* and *Dueñas* palaces in Seville are the best examples.

Happily Andalusian garden-making has entered its renaissance. In the revival a foreigner is playing a prominent part. We refer to the excellent work done by M. Forrestier, a Frenchman, who has worked with Spanish architects in laying out the new municipal park in Seville. Here and in other modern work, not only have they carried on the old tradition, but have introduced new ideas with taste and discretion.

The Andalusian garden is an urban, not a rural, creation. It exists in and near the towns. In Moorish days, the caliphs having accorded very special encouragement to agriculture and horticulture, the vegas of Granada, Cordova, Seville, Murcia, and Valencia had been converted from arid stretches into smiling orchards and gardens; but the Spaniards on conquering the same appear to have huddled in true medieval fashion close to the towns. The fields were abandoned. True, Christian fear of the hostile population was not unjustifiable, but even after the Mohammedans were driven from their last stronghold, Granada (1492), the vegas were not put under cultivation. Insecurity was then due to Christian nobles nourishing their feuds, and commoners living as highwaymen. Even when, in time, these conditions changed for better, the Spaniard seems to have had small inclination to be a country gentleman in the old Roman or modern English sense. He probably had his *villa rustica* to which he repaired in harvest time; this is perpetuated in the *cortijo* of the modern Andalusian, but it is a practical farm, not a mansion and garden. At any rate the old gardens that have survived are in, or close to, cities. In Seville we have the grounds of the *Alcazar;* overlooking Granada, the *Generalife.* Cordova's great garden, *Medinat-az-Zahra,* now but a memory, lay only three miles from the mosque; if it be true that the Cordova of the Caliphate was twenty miles in extent, then Medinat must have been within the city.

There are many reasons why the gardens of Andalusia should have so little in common with the rest of Europe. Merely to say that grass is not indigenous explains much; further, the climate is utterly dissimilar—heat, no frost, and but little moisture. Instead of every effort being made to catch and hold the sun's rays, to avoid them is the prime object. Plants and human beings must be cooled and shaded. Garden beds are sunken—real depressions; the raised flower bed so liked in France would wilt under an Andalusian sun. Water being far from abundant, there is no prodigal display of it.

Even with natural conditions less different, it is unlikely that the Mohammedan would have evolved anything resembling the vast English or French park or the highly architectonic villa garden of Italy. His attitude towards family life was reflected in his garden and in the Spanish derived from it. The Asiatic tendency to seclude women found its expression in a series of walled courts behind the house, not in a great open park surrounding it. Engravings of Andalusian gardens, had such been left to posterity, would not have been enlivened by richly dressed ladies lunching on the green and served by cavaliers on bended knee; nor would they show outdoor playhouses for children, nor "booths and tents to serve for the amusement of my lady and her guests." Such convivialities were appropriate north of the Pyrenees but not in Andalusia. Not recreation nor grandeur, but privacy, shade, fragrance, repose, were the desiderata.

Another Mohammedan tenet which had its effect on the garden was that figure sculpture, the chief embellish-

MEDINACELI PALACE, SEVILLE
Rear Garden

GARDENS OF THE GENERALIFE, GRANADA
Brick staircase serving three different terraces

GARDENS OF THE GENERALIFE, GRANADA
Upper Parterre

GARDEN OF HOUSE IN THE PLAZA DEL ALFARO, SEVILLE

GARDEN OF DON MIGUEL SANCHEZ DALP, SEVILLE
What one sees of sculpture today is posterior to the sixteenth century

GARDEN OF DON JOSÉ ACOSTA, GRANADA
Combining Spanish and Italian features

GARDEN OF THE UNIVERSITY, SEVILLE
Each enclosure is laid out with paths radiating from a central fountain

GARDENS OF THE ALCAZAR, SEVILLE

Garden walls are provided with recessed openings, giving pleasant vistas from one enclosure to another

GARDENS OF THE ALCAZAR, SEVILLE
One of the many stairs of polychrome tiles

ment of old Roman and Renaissance gardens, was forbidden to the Moor; what one sees of it to-day in Andalusia is posterior to the sixteenth century. The type of house also influenced the garden treatment—façade plain, all ornament being concentrated within to be admired by the owner and not by the passer-by. This being the case, the garden was not "architecturalized" out of all relation to the simple dwelling. In other words, the art of architecture was not confused with that of gardening. There were no tempiettos, exedras, imposing ramps, stairways; nor was the Andalusian, Moor, or Spaniard interested in the medieval *treillage* that the French Renaissance developed almost to excess. With an arcade, horseshoe or round, visible from his garden, he was content. In short, he used another alphabet. Even a similarity of climate between Spain and the country north of the Pyrenees could hardly have produced a Du Cerceau or a Le Nôtre.

Andalusian gardens are of two types, flat and hillside. Having said that gardens are to be sought in or near cities rather than forming part of isolated country seats, one need not be surprised to hear that the once great cities of Seville and Cordova on the broad banks of the Guadalquivir are the best centres for studying the flat garden; Granada and Ronda, high in the Sierra, for the hillside. There are only these two extreme types. Gently rolling stretches dotted with *bouquets d'arbres* do not enter into the scheme of Spanish topography.

The theory of the flat garden is a series of outdoor rooms walled apart by masonry and open to the sky; sometimes they are again subdivided by lower walls of hedge, or are quite roofed over by low-growing trees, always evergreens; in the centre almost invariably a fountain. The enclosures are referred to as *patios*, like that within the house, and are denominated according to the plant principally featured—patio of the orange trees, of the black bamboo, of the palm, of the box, etc. This conception of the garden, it will be seen, does not accommodate long alleys nor large pools of water. Squarish in form, the quadrangles rarely exceed forty feet to a side (we are speaking now of the private garden, not of a royal park like the Alcazar). Dividing walls are of white stucco and have, besides the connecting opening, several arched windows with grilles or rejas through which pleasant vistas can be had. Walks are either paved with glazed tiles or river pebbles, or are made of coloured earth tamped firmly down, an expedient also practiced by Italian and Dutch gardeners. Around the flower beds and circular openings for trees are borders of coloured tile. The object of this series of walled quadrangles is obvious; except for the few meridian hours of the day the walls, eighteen to twenty feet high, are casting their grateful shadow on either one side or the other.

Back of the garden for recreation was the *huerta*, for vegetables and fruit. Here rigid distinction was observed between the useful and the ornamental.

Flowers seldom intruded into its precincts. In contrast to the garden the *huerta* was quite devoid of shade—open to the sun to ripen quickly the successive crops of the year.

The hillside garden is an alternation of sequestered courts and open terracing, the topography determining which predominates. The site was chosen for its views townward, and afforded the Moorish gardener the opportunity to display that which he most excelled in—the arrangement and distribution of water. Here, too, walls played a great part, introduced even where not structurally necessary just because their white expanse was apparently considered an indispensable background. Outer or confining walls, especially if they surmounted an inaccessible cliff-side, were generally pierced with arched *clairvoyées* to reduce the distant view to a series of separate compositions. Another note of great interest was the stairway connecting the different levels—sometimes of azulejos, sometimes of unglazed flat tiles, sometimes of ordinary brick (the Roman type).

Both types of garden, flat and declivitous, were cheap to construct and to maintain. Even allowing for the cost of quarrying and terracing a hillside, the fact that no rich materials entered into its embellishment made it comparatively inexpensive—but little or no marble, no carved balustrading, no rusticated walls, no mosaics, no porphyry—all this meant much in the way of economy.

Another observation that applies to both types of garden is that green is a predominating note and that deciduous trees are practically absent. Among trees that hold their green the decorative and odorous citrous family were favourites; next came the more serious cypress and the low-growing box. The orange tree, needless to say, could always be bedded and was not planted in tubs as in less friendlv climates. It might be formally set out in round pockets and the circles connected by open conduits; or planted close so that the foliage formed a dense canopy; or plashed against the wall. Other fruit-bearing trees, though beautiful in flower, appear to have been ignored because of their naked season. The cypress of tall symmetrical habit and planted in pairs lent itself to training into an arch. Box was used prodigally, as it can be only in a garden where abundant bloom is not expected, for it, like the eucalyptus, consumes all the strength of the soil—box in form of hedges, box in isolated clumps, box in single bushes clipped into a sphere or other geometric form. Of elaborate topiary work there was none.

In this respect, as the Moor seldom fashioned the image of any living thing in the round, we may presume this to be his reason for avoiding an art familiar to the Persians and Egyptians, from whom, especially the former, the Moors borrowed extensively. The only attempt we have seen in an old garden at form and delineation in box is a parterre composed of the insignia of the great Spanish military orders, and this device must necessarily date from Christian not Moorish régime.

But if the Moor avoided the practice of topiary he was not averse to clipped evergreens in the form of

GARDENS OF THE ALCAZAR, SEVILLE
A cypress arch emphasizing the main walk

LAS ERMITAS, SIERRA DE CORDOVA
The cypress of tall symmetrical habit lends itself to arching

GARDEN OF THE MARQUES DE VIANA, CORDOVA
Gothic Arcade of Cedar

GARDEN OF THE MARQUES DE VIANA, CORDOVA
Wall openings overlooking the street

PARQUE DE MARIA LUISA, SEVILLE
A cypress arcade

QUINTA DE ARRIZAFA, CORDOVA
Brick steps from a lower to a higher enclosure

GARDENS OF THE ALCAZAR, SEVILLE
Manner of planting at the base of a wall

GARDENS OF THE ALCAZAR, SEVILLE
Brick path leading to the pavilion of Charles V

labyrinths. Box, cypress, myrtle, juniper, sometimes holly, were used, preference going to the aromatic greens. In fact, the maze so appealed to the oriental mind that hardly a garden was without one, though it might have been no more than twelve feet square. A specially fine maze formed part of the Alcazar gardens as originally laid out, but during one of the many changes wrought by the Emperor Charles V it was decided to uproot it and substitute an Italian parterre. The Emperor however appears to have fancied the Moorish maze sufficiently to deter its destruction until the plan had been carefully drawn up and baked into a tile panel; this tile was then embedded in the pavement of his little pavilion, where it may still be seen. The labyrinth is known to have been replanted elsewhere according to this plan, but only to again come to grief, for the one seen to-day at the extreme rear of the garden is of quite late date.

Flower beds are not of prime importance in the Spanish garden, flowering plants being displayed in pots and the colour scheme changed frequently. Every flower known to northerners grows in Andalusia, and in addition, the sub-tropical list; no month of the year is without its bloom. Roses and chrysanthemums when grown against a southern wall bloom all winter long. The amaranth is more graceful and feathery and vivid than we have seen it elsewhere; the cockscomb attains the proud length of eighteen inches; the geranium is of giant proportions as in Australia, and often pleached against a wall to a height of eighteen or twenty feet.

A weird exotic plant called *monstruo delicioso* has big, curiously perforated leaves and a long heavy tendril like coiled wire; though hardy-looking it requires much water.

Many of the exotic plants were brought to Spain by Abderrhaman I, first of the Omaiyad sultans, who was a great horticulturist and who sent to Syria and India for rare shrubs and seeds never before planted in European soil. It was this sultan who introduced the date palm into Spain; likewise the pomegranate (*la granada*), which, after the Christians wrested the Moorish kingdom of Granada from the Mohammedans, became a national emblem. According to the book of Abuzacaría (twelfth century), there had been brought into Spain jasmine and blue and yellow roses. The jasmine still perfumes the air, but the blue and yellow roses appear to have received no Christian encouragement.

Grass, tender, succulent grass such as makes the northern lawn, is unknown in Andalusia. If a few plots have been coaxed into life in the modern Seville gardens this is an exception due to special provision for watering them. The axiom "when at a loss what to plant use grass" did not help the Moorish gardener. But he devised another sort of green carpet — wandering Jew, ground ivy and myrtle, Iceland moss, hen and chickens, all planted thick and constantly snipped back into flatness. In this way a whole bed of green is obtained, as well as neat, orderly borders.

For the small flat garden the system of planting is

necessarily concentrated, since a large part of the area is given over to tiled pavement. The square, or patio, is laid out with paths, four to eight radiating from the central fountain. Borders may be of the green sort just described or of coloured tiles (azulejos) alone; or the strip of green may be confined within two rows of azulejos. The bed area is usually green save for one or two flowering plants; or it may be of black earth kept well turned and dotted with two or three plants; or more rarely it may be a flower bed all of one kind, thus giving a definite colour group. Where the green bed has a tree in its centre a generous circle of earth is left around the trunk and this earth is frequently hoed up in order to invite air and moisture into the soil.

This same general layout can be enlarged upon—box hedge, for instance, within a curb of tile or cement, lower border of dense ivy or myrtle, then turned-up earth, then shrubs, and finally the central circle for the tree. Each patio is a complete unit of pattern at small scale and capable of repetition, which, after all, is the underlying theory of all oriental design.

Where the patios of the flat garden are set out in rows of orange, magnolia, or pepper trees, the area is carefully lined off by irrigating furrows which are kept neatly banked. In the case of large trees like the magnolia (which here attains great size), a dense little grove of bamboo is planted under them, inviting by its additional coolness; or a bed of shade-loving plants.

It is interesting to examine the manner of planting

around the base of the dividing walls. A strip of earth about two feet wide is excavated to a foot or more below the level of the perimeter path, and down here, where their roots cannot raise the tiles or bricks of the walk, are planted the vines or trees that are to be pleached against the wall. Among the former are the bougainvillea, lantana (which here is both a large shrub and a vine), and the grape; among the latter, the orange, lemon, geranium, and the cypress, this kept well wired and clipped back flat to the wall. The interest of the cypress or other evergreens is enhanced by the patterns of the dark stems against the white stucco and the limited amount of green which is permitted to show itself. Where the purple or orange of flower or fruit enters into the decoration less attention is paid to the design of the stems. Of low planting against walls there was practically none. Considering that this space would be devoted to an herbaceous border of rich and varied bloom in an English garden, a greater difference in the two ways of treating it could hardly be imagined.

We have as yet said nothing about the walks that intersect the small units of the flat garden, and always in straight lines. Most often they are paved in tiles, and tiles as a garden embellishment will be taken up presently: but also, and with very *chic* effect, they are made of a bright ochre clay well rolled down. Between the yellow path and the black earth of the planted bed there is often a strip of reddish earth held in place by a tile edging or cement coping. This interesting and decorative

GARDENS OF THE ALCAZAR, SEVILLE
The theory of the flat garden is a series of walled enclosures open to the sky

GARDENS OF THE ALCAZAR, SEVILLE
Main pool at the highest level of the garden

PARQUE DE MARIA LUISA, SEVILLE
Brick rotunda adorned with tiles

GENERALIFE GARDENS, GRANADA
Green was the predominating note in the Spanish garden

GENERALIFE GARDENS, GRANADA
Pebbled pavement at entrance

GENERALIFE GARDENS, GRANADA
Stair with circular landings, water carried down the top of the parapet by means of a tiled runlet

GENERALIFE GARDENS, GRANADA
The site of the hillside garden was chosen for its views townward

use of coloured earths, renewing them frequently that they may look fresh, appears to be of Persian origin, and was revived in Europe in Renaissance gardens through the influence, probably, of Moorish Spain. Two attractive examples of the yellow clay paths are the *Convento de la Merced* garden and that of the Medinaceli palace, both in Seville.

Water, seen and heard, was a more indispensable part of the garden design than plants themselves. Arid Spain was made fertile by Moorish irrigation. The Moors were great hydraulicians, and what one sees to-day of scientific irrigation is but a miserably small fraction of what they left when driven out of the Peninsula. In using water as a decorative adjunct to the garden the scarcity of the supply influenced the manner of its application. A very little had to be made to look like a great deal. Artificial lakes therefore could not be dreamed of, nor even pools of any size with their aquatic plants and birds and their little islands connected by pretty toy bridges. Water was too precious to lie silent in a broad expanse; it had to be confined in terra-cotta canals and made to murmur through all its course. There was no periodical flooding of the entire area, nor wasteful flowing through earth ditches; instead, the thin stream was held to its course so that no drop escaped to nourish where not necessary. Diminutive conduits ran from tree to tree, from shrub to shrub. In the case of terraces, besides the open canal disappearing under the steps, the concave ramp of the stair itself might conduct water from an upper fountain to a lower. Whatever served this purpose, it was open and visible, and the water was made to show itself in as many places as possible before it was carried off to the more utilitarian *huerta*.

This endeavor to squeeze decorative benefit out of the last drop has resulted in special designing of fountains and basins. The pool of a spouting fountain, for instance, is not drained as it would be elsewhere; that is to say, there is not a waste below the rim of the basin, for then the effect of the play of water on the edge would be lost. As it is, it glides over, sparkles in the sun and increases the lustre of the tiles in so doing, then is caught in an outer gutter and carried off in an open canal. Basins of marble or stone have their outer brim faceted, by which device the volume of water spilling over seems augmented. Still another trick to produce the same illusion is to make the water reflect. Fountains are of glazed tile not merely because baked and enameled earthenware was a popular and inexpensive material, but also because its glazed surface makes a thin film of sunlit water gliding over seem greater in volume. Tiled paths are sprayed from minute jets not only to freshen and cool them but also to make them reflect and sparkle like a flowing stream.

These economical yet effective ways of using water in Spanish gardens offer a marked contrast to the copious *jets d'eau* and rushing cascades of the north (pathetically dry except on fête days). Wherever water has to be "used with due regardful thrift," the Andalusian way is worth studying. In our own southwest, where it costs more to water the garden than to heat the house, it offers a valuable suggestion; and, indeed, in more than the use of water, for the similarity of climate and growth also favors the Spanish tradition.

TWO UNITS OF A PATIO WALK LAID IN GREY AND WHITE PEBBLES, GRANADA

UBEDA
Postern gate in a small garden. Hood of green and white tiles

GENERALIFE GARDENS, GRANADA
Central canal of principal enclosure

GARDEN OF THE CASA DEL REY MORO, RONDA
Water carried in runlets from terrace to terrace

BAROQUE MARBLE FOUNTAIN, PALACE OF THE MARQUES DE PENAFLOR, ECIJA

THE ALHAMBRA, GRANADA
Marble fountain consisting of a Moorish tazza supported on a Renaissance pedestal

II

GARDEN ACCESSORIES

GARDENS OF THE ALCAZAR, SEVILLE
Insignia of the military orders planted in box in the sixteenth century

A GROUP OF SEVENTEENTH CENTURY ANDALUSIAN TILES

CHAPTER II

GARDEN ACCESSORIES

WE NOW come to the subject of garden embellishments. Sculpture being taboo, and elaborate architectonic treatment being incongruous with the simple exterior of the house, what then do we find in the way of accessories? The answer is brief: white stucco and polychrome tiles (*azulejos*). Modeled terra cotta is practically never used, and exposed brick but seldom; the proportion of paths and benches made of it is almost negligible beside those of tile. Stucco and glazed tile, at the same time ornamental and structural, vie with the planted elements.

The background of the whole garden arrangement is the stucco wall. It is rarely other than white. In Cordova colour was sometimes introduced in the shape of bands of blue or yellow kalsomine. Its surface is never purposely roughened—no striving for an undulating effect, for that comes of itself from repeated whitewashing.

The top of the wall is either flat, holding flowerpots, or it has a tile coping, or is made into a promenade with a parapet at each side. Doorways, generally arched, lead to other enclosures, which can also be viewed through window openings. These are provided with iron grilles and reveal seats laid in coloured tiles which in themselves are a handsome feature. The iron *reja* (grille) is again used at the doorway; also wood, either as a solid paneled door or worked into spindles. In Cordova the wooden gate is generally painted blue. A picturesque wall adjunct which one would like to meet more often is the gate hood, or *tejaroz*. These little eaves, covered with gutter tiles or with alternating green and white tiles glazed, are supported on carved pine corbels or on iron brackets. Sometimes it is a niche in the wall, instead of a gate, that is provided with a *tejaroz*. Such a niche probably held, in Moorish days, a decorative vase or a basin for ablutions, but the Spaniard refurnished it with a statue of the Virgin. Well niches, too, feature the wall, though generally the well is free-standing and in the patio of the house.

A detail that receives much attention is the pattern of the vine itself against the wall—clipped back to expose the trunk and its branching, and the foliage kept in well-studied patches.

In pretentious gardens, dividing walls serve also as a means of circulation, their thickness being sufficient to permit of a walk on the top, with protecting

Sections of various dividing walls surmounted by promenades

parapets. Arranged thus at the level of a second-story window or terrace of the house, they invite the inmates to promenade and survey the layout below. In the case of different levels these promenades are connected by stairs flanked by stepped parapets; while in the flat garden a variety of level is simulated by variety in the height of the walls, with connecting steps as described. This in itself lends much interest.

In the Alcazar gardens, Seville, a specially fine treatment may be seen. On the north side a heavy semi-fortified wall marking in part the original confines has a promenade and bench parapets on top, and is broken every hundred feet or so by a stout buttress whose top makes an agreeable little pavilion. Below, a shallow arcaded gallery is pierced in the thickness of the wall, like a triforium in the nave wall of a church. Open only on the south side overlooking the garden, this arcade is penetrated by the sun on its low winter arc and is at the same time shielded against the north wind; while in summer it is an equally agreeable promenade because it is always in shadow. A creation of Peter the Cruel, this was his favourite walk. As his Moorish builders left it — plain white stucco — it must have been dignified and beautiful; but centuries later it was made to suffer a revetment of coarsely vermiculated blocks. Some are in *yeso* (*stucco*) and the whole work is crude. Now the wall is neither Moorish nor Italian.

Enclosing a hillside garden on the side least accessible, the wall is often an open arcade for its whole length, thus extending the garden view to the country beyond. The recesses are provided with seats.

The other item which plays an important rôle in the Andalusian garden is baked earthenware in the form of azulejos and flower-pots, glazed and unglazed. The pots stand in never-ending lines much as if they had been arranged by children. Garden walks are edged with them, flower beds are designed with them, parapets are crowned with them. In ordinary cases they are the usual terra-cotta colour ; but when expected to form a part of a definite colour scheme they are painted and glazed accordingly, and take their place along with the polychrome tiles in the colour layout. Some fortunate gardeners are supplied with pots of several colours and this facilitates a complete change from time to time in the decorative scheme.

Decoration by means of polychrome tiles is the principal note of individuality in the Spanish garden. It is no exaggeration to say that colour is more often supplied by them than by flowers. Successfully to employ these coloured squares is an art in itself and the tyro cannot hope to acquire it at the first essay : it takes experience. To overdo is the temptation. Even with many good ancient examples before their eyes, the present-day advocates of the azulejo in modern Sevillian construction are using it on a lavish scale and with little discrimination. The principal objects made of azulejos were fountains, pools, benches, steps, and walks. In

DUCAL PALACE AT OSUNA
Garden Gate

LAS ERMITAS, SIERRA DE CORDOVA
The white-washed wall is the setting for every garden

TILED HOODS OVER GARDEN ENTRANCES, SEVILLE

PAVILION IN THE GARDENS OF MURILLO, SEVILLE
Typical profusion of potted plants. Pots and roof-tiles of alternate green and white

their construction flat tiles were used, never moulded as was the case in Italy.

The oldest Moorish tile decoration found is like a mosaic, slabs of solid colour having been tediously cut into small geometric shapes and fitted together to make the design. Later, two simpler processes were adopted: the first consisted in drawing the pattern on the wet square with grease and manganese, which made a dry line (*cuerda seca*) that prevented the colours from running together; the second meant pressing a metal matrix into the wet tile, the raised line thus formed acting as a barrier between the different colours. This process is named not for the line but for the hollow (*cuenca*) between. For a long time cuerda seca and cuenca tiles kept to geometric and floral designs, but after a while animal forms were added.

Early in the sixteenth century a monk from Pisa came to Seville and introduced free painting on tiles in the Della Robbia manner. *Pisanos* were soon turned out by the thousands and supplanted all others. A yellow ground was general with blue as the dominating note in the design. The Moorish tradition of geometric and small-scale floral patterns was thrown to the winds and decorative compositions in imitation of easel pictures became the vogue. In the baroque period such pictures (Murillo, of course, being a prime favourite) were incrusted in garden walls and protected by a *tejaroz* hood; even whole altars of tiles were set up in gardens, their devotional lamps suspended from the hood and twinkling in its shadow.

The making of azulejos is still the prime industry of Seville. Travellers who are interested may visit the chief factories in Triana, the ancient potters' *barrio* across the river. Here, besides garden vases, are made red, buff, and greenish unglazed tiles for the floor, and azulejos for wainscoting, paths, fountains, and benches—pressed, alas, by machines. The manufacturers are wise, probably, in seldom augmenting their pattern books by modern designs; and Andalusia and South America (to which there is a large exportation), equally wise in contenting themselves with the old Moorish and Renaissance motifs. It must be confessed that the greens and blues are not as rich and limpid as those which the sixteenth century knew how to produce, and that the new designs are sharp and the colours assertive beside tiles that have weathered three centuries; but there is no doubt that the new products will outlive this reproach. Those who want mellowness and delicacy in modern azulejos will have to wrestle hard with the manufacturer, who will argue, and quite aptly, that the fine old bits admired to-day in the Alcazar gardens were once as garish as any in his warerooms.

Considering first the tile fountain. Unlike its marble counterpart it is not meant to catch the eye from a distance, but to melt into the garden colour scheme. When combined with marble, as occasionally, the latter is subservient to the azulejos. Very often no part of the fountain except the actual jet rises above the level of the walk. The basin is shallow, six inches deep or so; it may be round, star-shaped, or octagonal, sunken or raised. As previously explained, the water is allowed to fall over the edge and is drawn off by an exterior gutter. In this manner the surface of the tiles is kept wet and their reflective power increased. By designing the squares for the botton of the basin in zigzags and interlacing curves the water appears to have more movement. If placed at the intersection of two paths paved also in polychrome such a fountain loses much of its decorative value; it should be considered somewhat like a stone to be set in a brooch. Best seen from a height, the flat fountain is the type most employed in patios and garden enclosures that can be looked into from a promenade wall. Sometimes the entire fountain is sunken, looking deeper and cooler therefore. The finest of this sort is in the patio of the asylum for retired priests (*Los Padres Venerables*) in Seville. Here the basin and fountain are of marble, the surrounding treatment of tiles.

Corresponding more in design to the typical European conception is the raised fountain, but being executed in tiles it is devoid of moulded sections. In general, it consists of a raised brim, often octagonal, and a central shaft and smaller basin of marble. Bearing out our suspicion that the Christians were more prone than the Moors to the use of coloured tiles, is the fact that nearly every raised fountain in the Alhambra is of marble alone. Similar to the tiled fountain but smaller in diameter is the well-curb of the house patio. The

Moors had beautiful well-curbs of glazed pottery in one piece, generally grey-green, ornamented with raised patterning and inscriptions, but these are seen to-day only in museums, not in gardens. Clever facsimiles are made by certain Andalusian ceramic factories and sold as originals to tourists.

Almost as numerous as the fountain is the tiled bench. Here, too, form is determined by the material, the bench being completely solid, with the face under the seat set back at an angle to accommodate the feet of the occupant. The seat has a slight pitch to throw off the water. Without a back the tiled bench is more graceful, particularly if free-standing; but where there is a back its rigidity can be modified by embedding it in a hedge. Another type of bench is that projecting from a wall, its tiled back set flush with the stucco surface. The back is generally carried much higher than is necessary to protect one from the whitewash, and the upright panel is framed in a border of solid colour. By this arrangement bench and wall help each other decoratively, as the illustration of the Osborne garden shows (*Calle de Guzman el Bueno*, in Seville).

The bench, like the fountain, is generally very colourful. Old ones may be seen in the Alcazar gardens made of Pisanos, yellow background, green and blue painting. Backed up by dense masses of box, the colour is rich and full of quality, but it must not be forgotten that much of the charm lies in the mellowness of the old tiles. To one experimenting with

HOUSE IN THE CALLE GUZMAN EL BUENO, SEVILLE
Garden Accessories in Polychrome Tile

LARGE STEPPED POOL IN POLYCHROME TILES
ASYLUM FOR AGED PRIESTS (LOS VENERABLES), SEVILLE

POOL LINED WITH BRICK AND POLYCHROME TILES, THE ALCAZAR, SEVILLE

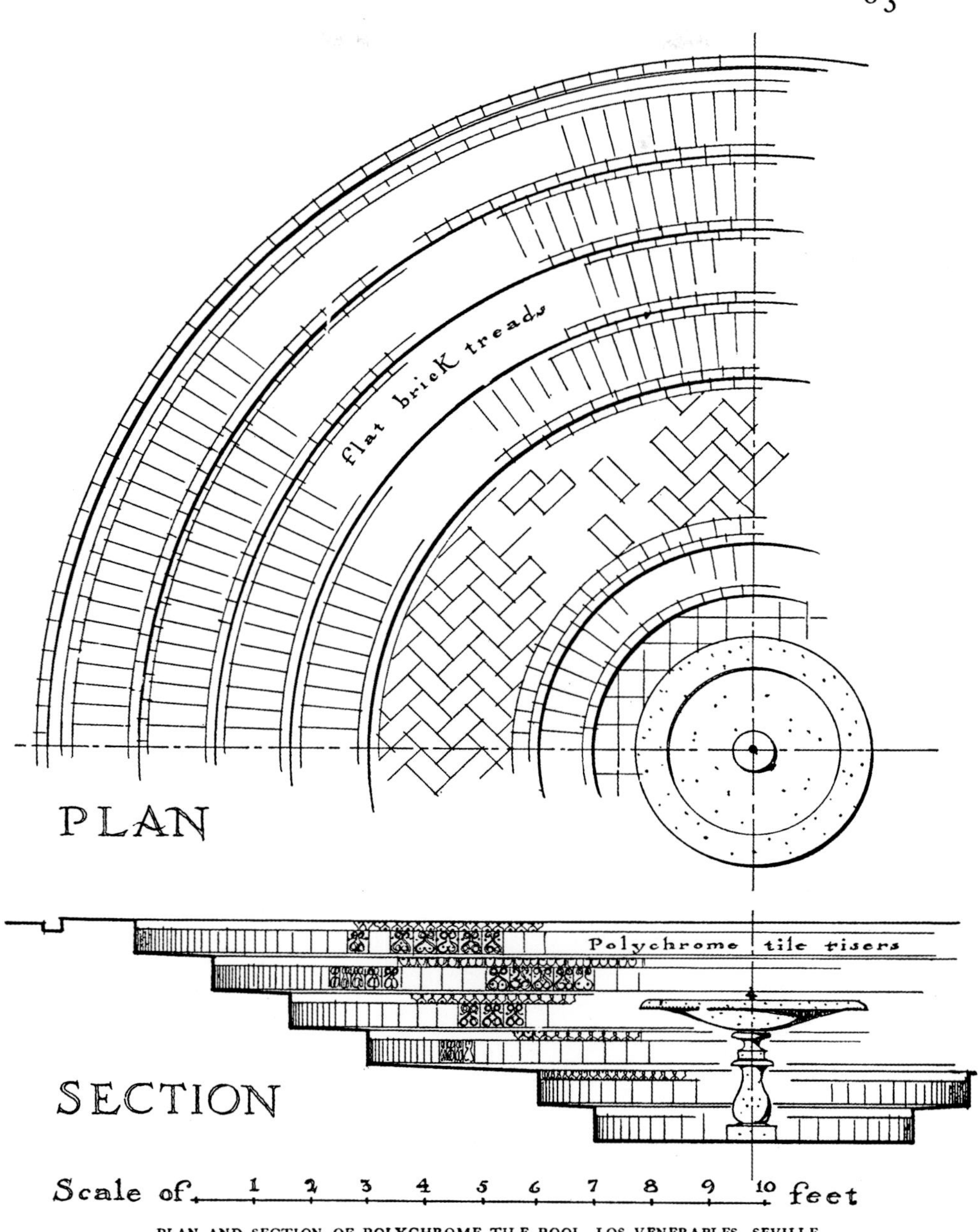

PLAN AND SECTION OF POLYCHROME TILE POOL, LOS VENERABLES, SEVILLE

TILED PATIO AND HOODED WELL WITH EARTH POCKETS AT THE SIDE FOR PLANTING, SEVILLE

DIMINUTIVE PATIO GARDEN WITH BRICK EXEDRA, SEVILLE

GARDEN ENTRANCE, SEVILLE, SHOWING USE OF TILED HOODS OVER OPENINGS this material it soon becomes evident that effects can be obtained with old tiles that would be less pleasing with new. Sixteenth- and seventeenth-century units of every conceivable colour may be assembled with admirable results, whereas if the tiles were new considerable restraint would have to be practiced. Good modern benches are seen in the *Parque de Maria Luisa* in Seville—unglazed terra cotta coloured tiles with brilliant polychrome insets in the form of escutcheons or flower panels.

In the matter of tiled walks one must be cautious; to create a too interesting pavement is a great temptation. The best old examples consist of unglazed oblongs measuring about five by eight inches, laid in basket-weave with a small coloured inset filling the interstices. This little two-inch square is decorated with some very simple device—the lion of Leon, the castle of Castile, the pomegranate of Granada, the *nudo* or knot of Seville, or a personal coat-of-arms. But the basket-weave precedent has been followed in wholesale fashion in modern Sevillian work, prompting the question whether it is not possible to overdo even a good thing. Besides, in the old work there was more sense of relative fitness; secondary gardens and patios were not treated in the same quality of material and the same design as the more important units, and it is precisely this discrimination that one misses in the Seville revival. The architect lights upon an attractive pattern or layout and makes it serve through the whole house and garden with but little varying of design, and none at all of quality or quantity.

Another method practiced in the old gardens to enliven monotone unglazed paths was to concentrate rich colour in an occasional panel the full width of the walk—geometric, floral, or heraldic. Even old broken tiles have been gathered up and laid mosaic fashion to form such a panel with good results. The insets are not regularly spaced, and their lack of formality is a relief after visiting a modern garden whose every path is laid in the basket-weave just described.

Paths are further decorated by tile curbs of attractive colour; or by narrow tiled conduits passing through their centre. Curbs are generally of a single colour or of white alternating with a single colour; and the bottom of the little canal is often thus laid so that it too contributes to the scheme.

In the gardens of the Alcazar and dating from the time of Charles V (1516-1556) there is a charming little pavilion treated in polychrome tiles. Such a feature is a departure from Moorish precedent. Pavilions and gazebos formed no part of the Andalusian design; not even a tool-house to invite decorative treatment, for the custom was and still is to store all implements in the vaulted chambers underneath the house. Charles V's pavilion is square, arcaded on all sides, and has a rich dado of polychrome tiles. Inside walls are similarly treated; some of metallic lustre, and very precious. The ceiling is a *media naranja* (half orange) or typical

Moorish wooden dome, while the outside roof is of ordinary gutter-tiles but with every fifth ridge glazed in blue and white. Instances of this sort show that the Spanish garden can be made more catholic in taste without losing its special *cachet*.

In planning an Andalusian garden it is well to follow a definite colour arrangement. As said before, more colour is supplied by the tiles than by the flowers. A fairly large garden might have all its bordering in alternate blue and white, or yellow and white; very effective is a combination of black and white. A study of the oldest examples shows that not nearly so many colours were assembled in one enclosure as modern gardeners are inclined to use.

Colour tiles are also applied to the construction of garden stairs, the colour confined to the riser, while the nosing and tread are of unglazed earth colour; the same type of stair is common in patios. A stair extending between two terraces is made broad enough to accommodate a border of flower-pots on each side.

Almost as ubiquitous as the tiled walk is that of river pebbles laid in patterns—an attractive mosaic of deep purple, grey, and white. The effectiveness of this simple medium is surprising. It was not considered too cheap or commonplace even for royal precincts, as witnesses the magnificent pebble escutcheon of Charles V in front of his fountain in the Alhambra Park. No Moorish example however is as elaborate as this, for in pebble pavements, as in all other bits of design, geometric patterns were the rule. Pebbles are also used for garden steps, in combination with stone nosing. Sometimes the white unit is supplied by sheeps' knuckles, but this, for some reason we have not investigated, is more general in the cloisters of Carthusian convents than in gardens. Occasionally the stones are laid flat, but as a rule they are set on edge and well grouted in cement.

The Andalusian garden is essentially a well-kept garden. In physiognomy it is like the Andalusian himself, who is clean-shaven, close-cropped, even to cutting back the hair from the temple to a rigid straight line. His garden is not a sentimental spot with old-fashioned flowers running riot; no "sweet confusion;" none of the picturesque beauty of the English St. Catharine's Court. Just a smallish retired spot, not costly, yet very sure of its place among gardens and proud of its ancient lineage, for it was created when the rest of western Europe was still semi-barbarous.

BENCH EXECUTED IN POLYCHROME TILE

BENCH EXECUTED IN POLYCHROME TILE

BENCH EXECUTED IN POLYCHROME TILE

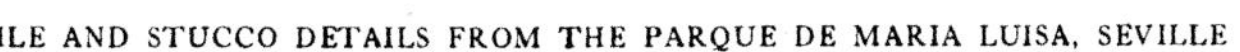

TILE AND STUCCO DETAILS FROM THE PARQUE DE MARIA LUISA, SEVILLE

III

PATIOS OF CORDOVA, SEVILLE, AND GRANADA

FORMER PALACE OF THE ALTAMIRAS, SEVILLE
An open corridor treated in stucco, coloured tiles, and green woodwork

CHAPTER III

PATIOS OF CORDOVA, SEVILLE, AND GRANADA

ALL northerners agree with Théophile Gautier that "the Andalusian patio is a charming institution." Indoor garden, with growing plants and vines in its open centre; outdoor parlour, with chairs and tables and vargueño cabinets and pictures under its roofed arcades. In both humble and pretentious houses the patio was the nucleus of the plan; it answered to climatic conditions, also to the Moorish tradition of sequestered family life. Andalusia underwent a change of régime from Mohammedan to Christian; but the climate was not affected thereby, nor was this belief in seclusion, and so the Moorish plan was retained. Accepting further the Arab idea of a plain exterior and a rich interior, it was the patio rather than the façade of the house that the Spaniard embellished.

The two stories of the patio are connected by an enclosed stair running up between walls and opening directly off the patio without hall or vestibule. In the sixteenth century the Renaissance type with open stairwell made its appearance in Spanish domestic architecture but was coldly received. Builders, even of palaces, went on with the inclosed stair—its treads of plain tiles, risers of polychrome, and protective nosing formed of a heavy billet of oak, square in section. Stucco and tile wainscot made the walls; tiles, the well and pavement, save perhaps for small corner flower-beds; the surrounding arcade was generally ornamented in *yeseria* (carved adamantine stucco), and its ceiling was of pine beams painted in the Moorish manner. In the case of a small house with one patio, the well stood in the corner most accessible to the kitchen. In larger patios the garden feature of a central fountain was often introduced. The well parapet is generally of tiles and the arch for the pulley is either of iron or stone. Standing around, to complete the picture, are a few carrying jars of graceful form either in copper or glazed earthenware.

Planting is limited to vines and trees which grow from earth pockets at the base of the arcade piers, and which are trained to form a leafy ceiling over the whole court; but though there are no flower-beds to speak of, potted plants are used without number, and of infinite variety are the designs and the colour-schemes in which they are set out.

Cordova, Seville, and Granada, the three most important Andalusian cities either in the past or the present, evolved each a distinct sort of patio, though now, as will be explained presently, the Sevillian type is dominant. The *Cordoveses*, caring less about tiles than did the *Sevillanos* or the *Granadinos*, satisfied their colour sense by kalsomining their white patio walls with bands of ultramarine, ochre, or green—rather sparingly. Sometimes the piers supporting the second story were painted; in the Viana patio they are bright yellow, and the glazed flower-pots match. Architecturally the Cordovan patio was less developed than the others—square stucco or stone

PATIO OF THE FORMER ALTAMIRA PALACE, SEVILLE
For the well-head and wall-borders polychrome tiles are used

PATIO OF THE FORMER ALTAMIRA PALACE, SEVILLE
Polychrome tiles are most effective when sparingly used

PATIO STAIR AND WELL-HEAD, MONDRAGON PALACE, RONDA
Varying levels characterize the Spanish groundfloor

CASA CHAPIZ, GRANADA
Typical sixteenth century Granadine patio showing Mudejar woodwork

CLOISTER OF THE CONVENTO DE SANTA CLARA, MOGUER
Whitewashed walls, a brilliant polychrome well, and scant planting

CASA CHAPIZ, GRANADA
A secondary patio with gallery supported on corbels instead of columns

A TYPICAL SEVILLIAN PATIO TREATED IN TILES

piers upholding the arcade, or even, instead of arches, a plain post-and-lintel construction. Pebble pavements in black and white abound. There is much charm in these simple patios—bright patches of sun, exquisite bluish shadows, and one vivid colour.

Besides the Viana patio, which is shown when the family are not in residence, that of the *Museo Provincial* is another typical example. This house, once a palace, has in addition a charming little second-story loggia with a facing of azulejos. Another house is entered from this same patio. It has a pretty informal garden at the back, full of fragrant flowers and adorned with fine fragments of Moorish carving dug up nearby—débris of what was the one centre of culture in Western Europe during the Dark Ages.

The Sevillian patio is much more "dressy." Its owners kindly permit the passer-by to get a glimpse of it from the street through the iron grille (*reja* or *cancilla*) of its vestibule. It is primarily an expression in coloured tiles and white ornamental plasterwork. Whether its Moorish prototype gave so much space to the polychrome tile is doubtful, it being quite likely that Christian Seville took to this manner of display only after it waxed rich through being the official port for trade with the New World; at any rate, residents of Cordova claim that their simple patio is truer to the Moorish. In this matter of introducing colour it is rather anomalous that the Christian Spanish should have wanted more of it in the form of tiles, and yet always left white the carved stucco which the Moor painted so gaily—overpainted, we are apt to think after walking through the royal Moorish palace of the Alhambra.

Aside from its exuberance of azulejos the Sevillian patio is further distinctive in being more architectural—marble columns to its arcade, an enclosed upper story with pedimented windows looking down into the court, a designed fountain instead of, or supplementing, a well. Many of the painted wooden ceilings over the patio-galleries date from the sixteenth and seventeenth centuries and were the work of Moors. In this same epoch a great deal of marble was used for pavements, and handsome iron rejas were ordered for patio windows. Another feature of interest is the panelled door — Moorish carpentry — that gives access to the various rooms opening from the patio; also the manner of hanging it — instead of being hinged in a jamb it stands forward of the opening and is pivoted top and bottom, the socket of the top embedded in a projecting corbel of either wood or stone. Altogether the Sevillian patio is a very attractive outdoor living-room and is well worth the attention of American architects; not only those of Florida and the southwest, where there is a Spanish tradition to live up to, but those in any part who are called on to build summer homes. The application of coloured tiles is now past the experimental stage; and the carved stucco duro, or *yeseria*, could be admirably interpreted in terra cotta.

It is hardly necessary to indicate the notable patios

of Seville, beautiful ones being visible or partly so in any street outside of the shopping district. Besides the well-known palaces of the Duques de Alva and Medinaceli (who seldom reside in them) there is the contemporaneous Pinelos house at No. 6, Abades, which is now a pension, and the Olea, in Guzman el Bueno. This last has been occupied for over a century by an English family, the Osbornes. Nearly all the houses on this street possess patios quite as fine. For picturesque but dilapidated examples one must prowl about the old Jewry—*Calle Levies* and all around *Santa Maria la Blanca*, the former synagogue, where rich Jews built their palaces; while in another quarter, opposite *San Juan de la Palma*, is the former Altamira palace, now rented out in studios and its paved patio serving as a warehouse for antique dealers.

The Granada patio is thoroughly Mudéjar, that is to say, of Moorish work but executed for Christians. More accurate would it be to say that it is thoroughly Moorish, for there is no evidence that it underwent any modification whatever on being taken over by the Spaniards. Structurally it is much lighter than the Sevillian. Wood, not stone, was the material employed; that is, while there were still Moorish carpenters in Granada to fashion it, but after their breed had gone the Granadine patio took on more the aspect of the Sevillian. Of the two stories, the upper was also a covered gallery and had a rail of wooden spindles, while the lower or supporting story was rarely an arcade, but instead, a post-

and-lintel construction. Delicate marble colonnettes, hexagonal piers of brick stuccoed, or carved wooden corbels, bore the weight. The beamed ceilings covering the walks were not painted in polychrome, but the beam ends, projecting to form the eaves, were carved in oriental fashion into a curious fish or animal head. Doors opening onto the patio were panelled and moulded, making that combination of rectangular panels of varying size that later became known as the "sacristy door." The rails of the second-story balustrade were square, set at an angle and fluted or reeded. Pebble pavements are more used in Granada than elsewhere, and the vines that are trained to screen the open quadrangle often grow from huge *tinajas*, or oil jars such as Morgiana shut the forty thieves in. While the Granada patio remained true to the precedent of well-carved, oiled woodwork in combination with plain stucco walls, it was the most distinctive of the Andalusian types, but in the seventeenth century, after the exodus of the Moors, columnar arcades took the place of wooden galleries, the open Renaissance stair began to supplant the narrow enclosed stair of tile and wood, and the patio lost its picturesque, sympathetic note. Easy to visit are the *Casa Chapiz* and a similar one in the *Horno de Oro*, just declared a *Monumento Nacional*.

The patio, it will be seen, corresponds to the Italian cortile, but the treatment we have just described made of it a much more domestic-looking feature. It is the summer living-room of all Andalusian families; in

PATIO OF THE HOSPICIO, FORMERLY EL CONVENTO DE LA MERCED, CORDOVA

PATIO OF THE HOSPICIO, CORDOVA
Typical Cordovan Baroque treated in white and yellow stucco

AN OLD CORDOVA PATIO WITH COLOURED TILE WINDOW TREATMENT

FIFTEENTH–CENTURY CLOISTER, CONVENTO DE SANTA CLARA, MOGUER
The Andalusian cloister was the prototype for the early American missions

FORMER MONASTERIO DE SAN JERONIMO, SIERRA DE CORDOVA
Gothic cloisters now form part of the villa of the Marques del Merito

THE ABANDONED CARTUJA AT JEREZ
The once beautiful cloister now serves as a grazing ground

winter they move upstairs. During the seventeenth century, when the surcharged baroque style came to Spain, palaces then erected or remodelled received formal patios that could never take on the lived-in quality of the typical patio. Baroque, however, found its patrons chiefly among the rich monasteries — especially those of the Jesuits — so that in the domestic field the number of richly treated patios is small. That of the Marques de Peñaflor in Ecija is one of the finest examples in Andalusia. Among religious houses the "*Compañía*" (Jesuits) in Cordova is specially sumptuous, while the former *Convento de la Merced*, now the Hospital, combines baroque with the traditional stucco and kalsomine trimming.

In the cloisters of Andalusia as well as in the more ancient ones of northern Spain we find an interesting type of garden. To the inmates of a religious asylum the cloister meant even more than the patio did to the members of the family, and to its planting and care they gave much attention. It was not only a *hortus conclusus;* it was also the one passage leading to the various departments of the institution, a veritable thoroughfare in its small way. Into its covered walks opened the chapel, the chapter-house, the refectory, the library, etc.

The first religious communities had in their struggling period but one cloister — a single-storied arcade with a wooden lean-to roof, this often vividly painted in the Moorish tradition. The columns were set in pairs, that is, two deep according to the thickness of the arch soffit. As the monastic institution waxed richer and more important, it added a second story to its cloister, or even had two such enclosures. The walks were ceiled with masonry vaulting, and rich carved ornament was introduced into the capitals of the arcade. This display of art, especially of the human figure, was disapproved of by Saint Bernard, and his order, the Cistercian, returned to leaf and geometric patterns; but later, in Gothic days, all restrictions were ignored and the tracery and capitals of all cloisters became very ornate.

As to the open or garden part there were two essential items—the sombre cypress and the utilitarian well. This last was usually the centre from which radiated the pattern, but the Cistercians covered, or rather surrounded, the well with a handsome well-house, and changed its position to one side, that opposite the refectory door. Here the monks stopped for ablutions before going to meals. Such a lavatory, hexagonal, was *de rigueur* in the cloisters of the order, and particularly fine ones can be seen at Poblet and Santas Creus, near Barcelona. In late cloisters of the fifteenth and sixteenth centuries the central well was enclosed in a sort of tempietto, as at El Paular and Guadalupe. In the latter, there is not only an elaborate brick well-house in the centre, but also a lavatory in one corner, though the order that built it was the Hieronymite, not the Cistercian. The cloister well-curb was generally of marble and surmounted by a fine wrought-iron head for the pulley. Walks were of gravel, stone flags, pebbles combined with sheep knuckles, or of glazed tiles; curbs for garden-beds were of stone. In the garden proper there were no benches, but on the inner or covered side of the arcade parapet ran a stone bench.

Cloister gardens having stood abandoned during the half-century of disestablishment of the religious orders, and only a few of them ever having been rehabilitated, their planting-scheme is no longer trim and easily appreciated. It was never elaborate. Four or six paths, box-lined, led from the centre, these crossed by subsidiary walks where the area was large, in which case the beds occupied less space than the intersections. Flowers were specially chosen for their perfume, and roses and lilacs still make the air heavy in many an abandoned cloister.

It was the Andalusian cloister that served as model for the monks who built the missions in our own southwest. With its white sun-beat walls instead of the sombre cold masonry of the north, and its polychrome tiled pavements instead of dark-grey flagstones, it imparted a decidedly more cheerful note to monastic life. Of this type the cloister of the convent of Santa Clara in Moguer (a few miles from Palos, whence Columbus set sail on his immortal voyage) is the popular expression. Enormously thick walls with cooling, shadow-inviting reveals—walls so often whitewashed that detail has become indiscernible; a well in the centre with curb of battered polychrome tiles and a decorative iron head;

planting confined to a few pleached orange trees and vines; potted flowering plants guarded under the arcade away from the blazing sun—this white cloister seen through the iron grille by moonlight has a very rare and special beauty.

Among the monasteries bought and converted into residences since the Disestablishment may be mentioned that of San Jerónimo in Cordova, another of the same order in Lupiana, near Guadalajara, the former belonging to the Marques del Mérito and the latter again for sale; the Benedictine of San Benet de Bages, home of the painter, Don Ramon Casas; and the Carthusian of Valdemosa, Majorca, where Georges Sand and her lover, Chopin, lodged shortly after the monks left, and which was recently acquired by the late illustrious Catalan bibliophile and scholar, Don Isidor Bonsems. In all these cases the abandoned and overgrown cloister was replanted and given the domestic touch of the family patio, and a more pleasing form of small intimate garden would be hard to find.

CLOISTER OF THE MONASTERIO DE NUESTRA SEÑORA DE GUADALUPE
To build this artizans were summoned from Andalusia by the Abbot

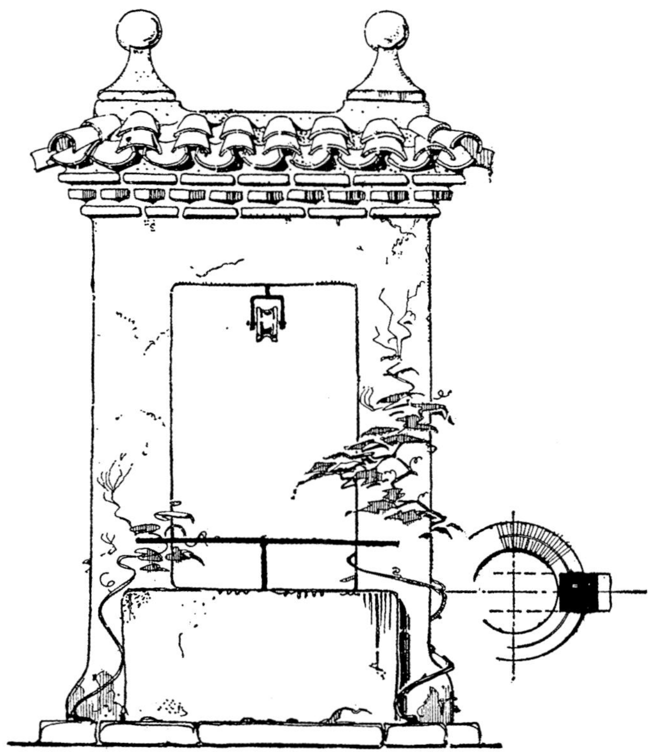

A WELL-HEAD OF BRICK AND STUCCO, ECIJA

IV

THE GARDENS "DEL REY MORO," RONDA, AND LAS ERMITAS, SIERRA DE CORDOVA

CHAPTER IV

THE GARDENS "DEL REY MORO," RONDA, AND LAS ERMITAS, SIERRA DE CORDOVA

DEL REY MORO

IN RONDA, a few hours by rail north of Gibraltar, is a *chef-d'oeuvre* in the way of a small hillside garden. The *Casa del Rey Moro* (House of the Moorish King, according to local legend) is now the property of the Duchess of Parcent, by whom the old white villa and its garden have been most admirably reclaimed.

The city of Ronda, magnificently surrounded by lofty mountain ranges, is built on an isolated ridge which is rent asunder from base to top by the deep narrow chasm of the Guadalevin River. Clinging to the south side is the primitive Moorish town; spreading out on the opposite, the more modern Christian quarter which sprang up after the city was captured from the Moors by Ferdinand and Isabella in 1485. It would be on the south side, then, that we should look for Moorish remains. The several interesting white villas along the gorge or *tajo*, once belonged to Mohammedan nobility—even to royalty, as is popularly claimed; among their Spanish possessors are the Marques de Salvatierra, the Marques de Parada, and the Duquesa de Parcent. Only this last is the fortunate owner of a garden. To construct it the French expert Forrestier was called in. Because of the nature of the ground he had to become something of an inventor.

As seen by the drawing, the site presented great difficulties. It is a precipice rather than a hillside. The modern landscape architect could not be satisfied with merely quarrying for a foothold, but wrested from the rock sufficient terrain to accommodate a neat scheme, a small garden so ingeniously arranged that one gets an impression of actual amplitude. In the uppermost part he had to do much filling-in; in the cliffside, much tunnelling, stepping, and terracing to add beauty and interest. Here he found a stair cut in the rock down to the river-bed and left it as it had been ever since the problem of securing water was thus solved by the *Rey Moro's* architect. As one looks down from the garden proper, the various little footholds, walled-in and planted or paved with tiles, make agreeable oases in the rocky side of the gorge.

The garden-plot measures some fifty by one hundred and seventy-five feet, the house being at the highest point and to the east. This area would be insignificant elsewhere, but here, as said, is made to look spacious. Conforming to the declivity westward, three levels were created. That adjacent to the house is treated in the strictly Andalusian manner—nearly all tiled; the intermediary, as the garden proper, with considerable planting; the lowest, while made to conform strictly to the topography, is composed to serve as the culmination of the composition. From the fountain of the uppermost area, a typical little four-inch open conduit, tile-lined, passes down the various levels and terminates in a pool.

Commanding as it does not only the rest of the garden but also the white town backed by a sweeping panorama of exceptional grandeur, this uppermost level had to be provided with seats. These are of tile, their brilliant yellow and blue making a splendid colour note against the dense mass of shrubbery; thus set, the rigid contour of the free-standing tile bench with back is made more agreeable. On the north side, overlooking the chasm and the town, is a pergola of one bay, while along the south or street wall is a continuous pergola dropping down the three levels and making a sheltered walk along the whole length of the garden; this arbor is supported on stone columns with coarsely carved capitals. Planting in the highest part is restricted to a few well-grouped plots cleanly defined by clipped box; the rest is paved with unglazed flat bricks in basket-weave with small coloured insets. The basin of the fountain, the canal, and the coping of the foliage beds, are all in polychrome; the font itself is of marble.

Seven feet below and reached by a balance stair with a grotto between is the flower-garden—two sizable beds edged with box trimmed at intervals into pyramids. Rose-bushes and diminutive shrubs make up the planting. The walks are of gravel. This being a circulating space, there are no seats.

The lowest level, screened at the back by cypresses, is more secluded. It, too, is reached by a balance stair, but here circular and embracing a tile-lined pool. The paths that radiate from here form with their various termini the rest of the scheme. The well-head placed on the main axis came from a Renaissance palace. Well, exedras, cypresses—all are reminiscent of Italy, yet adjust themselves admirably to the topical treatment of the upper parts of the scheme.

Fully to appreciate this charming little garden one must keep the designer's problem in mind; his available area was very reduced; one side was bounded by a gorge, the other three by a congested semi-Moorish town; breathing-space, privacy, and an impression of perspective and distance had to be secured, hence the extreme motivation. More highly developed in plan than the average Andalusian garden, it instantly announces that the designer could not wholly reconcile himself to traditional Andalusian simplicity. His French sense of design had to assert itself. Yet aside from the pergola and exedra, in favour of which tradition may well be ignored at times, all the embellishment is oriental—solid parapets instead of the balustrade, low pools instead of the raised fountain, brick and glazed tile instead of marble, areas of tiled pavement instead of grass, and vegetation dwarfed and restrained instead of natural. The architect has, one may say, carried the Andalusian tradition forward into the twentieth century, modernizing it for the needs of a twentieth-century cosmopolitan family.

LAS ERMITAS, SIERRA DE CORDOVA

We have mentioned Cordova, the city, as a natural region to look for flat gardens; but to the west of the town, mounting into the Sierra de Cordova where once

GARDEN OF THE CASA DEL REY MORO
The upper terrace commanding a view over the gorge to the town of Ronda

THE MIDDLE GARDEN TERRACE, CASA DEL REY MORO
White retaining walls and amphorae of brilliant colors

GARDEN PLAN, CASA DEL REY MORO

THE LOWEST TERRACE, CASA DEL REY MORO
The formal terrace with free planting and gravel walks

DETAIL OF THE POOL, CASA DEL REY MORO
Executed in glazed white tiles

LOOKING UP THE THREE GARDEN LEVELS TOWARDS THE VILLA, CASA DEL REY MORO

PATIO OPENING ON TO THE GARDEN, CASA DEL REY MORO

ENTRANCE TO THE MONASTERY CALLED LAS ERMITAS (HERMITAGE)
In the Sierra de Cordova

stood fine Moorish villas and gardens, are a few hillside examples of interest. One of these, *El Convento Ermitaño*, we illustrate. It occupies a site favoured by hermits ever since the remote introduction of Christianity into Spain. This high-lying convent (in Spanish, convent and monastery are synonymous) is inhabited by a dozen old monks, each living separately in his little white *casita* and keeping his hillside patch of green in order. It is the layout of these individual quarters that is specially attractive—all white stucco against which the simple planting is very effective. The well-cared-for slopes are covered with luxuriant olive trees, and in the gardens proper are tall cypresses and stone pines, which make the various small hermitages appear all the more diminutive and homelike.

On the return to Cordova one may visit the *Quinta de Arrizafa*, supposed once to have been an estate of Abderrhaman, first of the great caliphs. Mediocre as to garden craft, it is interesting for its extraordinary prodigality of flowers; there is also a famous aviary of pheasants and fighting cocks.

ENTRANCE TO THE CHAPEL FORECOURT, LAS ERMITAS
Through an arch of cypresses

LAS ERMITAS. THE MONASTERY GROUP
Chapel and separate *casitas*, a study in green and white

LAS ERMITAS. A HILLSIDE OF ORANGE AND OLIVE TREES TERRACED WITH WHITE WALLS

LAS ERMITAS, WHERE EACH HERMIT IS RESPONSIBLE FOR HIS OWN GARDEN PLOT

LAS ERMITAS. EACH STRUCTURE AND GARDEN IS SURROUNDED BY A HIGH WHITE WALL

V

THE GENERALIFE, GRANADA

VIEW FROM THE LOFTY MIRADOR SHOWING GRANADA AND THE ALHAMBRA IN THE DISTANCE

THE PRESENT DAY APPROACH TO THE GENERALIFE GARDENS

CHAPTER V

THE GENERALIFE, GRANADA

GRANADA is a mountain city three thousand feet above sea level. Sentimental tourists who go to it steeped in the literature of the Romantic School are generally disappointed. It is difficult for them to picture the empty, over-restored royal courts peopled with languishing Moorish maidens, or to see the ragged, importuning gypsy women as haughty beauties with slumbering fire in their eyes; consequently they feel that Granada has somehow not come up to their expectations.

As a matter of fact few cities in the world can compare with it for sheer beauty of situation. Of that at least the change of owners could not deprive it. Little is left of the Moors' Capital except the *Alhambra* on the acropolis and the *Generalife* on the opposite hill. Of the many sumptuous palaces, villas, and gardens of the Moorish aristocracy that occupied the Albaicin and other surrounding hills, not a trace is left; but when the conquering Spaniards entered in the first days of the year 1492 they must have beheld a display of hanging gardens such as met the unaccustomed eye of the rugged warrior from Macedon when he entered Babylon. To-day we are reduced to the two examples mentioned above.

The Generalife, supposed to have been the summer residence (*Casa de campo*) of the Granada kings, was probably built in the late fourteenth century. It owes its preservation to its having been given, along with a Christian beauty, as a suitable reward to an aristocratic Moor who turned Christian. Legend further states that it never passed from their descendants. Until recently the Generalife, also the interesting sixteenth-century palace known as the *Casa de los Tiros* down in the city, was held by the Marqueses de Campotejar, who, through remote intermarriage with a Genoese family, changed their nationality and spent but little time in their Spanish ancestral residences. Between them and the Spanish crown a suit for possession of these two Granada properties was pending for over a century, to be settled only last year in favour of Spain. The town house is to become a museum, and the Generalife is to be restored as a public garden. If only the work receives the wise supervision of the *Comisario Regio* who is urging the scheme on the government (the Marques de Vega Inclan), we may hope to see the feeble cast-iron fountains, railings, and other intrusions of the nineteenth century replaced by appropriate reproductions of Moorish originals. Beyond this and the clipping back of the overgrown foliage which now disguises much of the layout but little is to be done, unless it be to reopen the original entrance to the grounds. What the seventeenth century left in the gardens is picturesque and not incongruous.

We have here a fine example of an old hillside garden, the more valuable because it can be studied in relation to the villa which formed part of the scheme. All the architectural units being practically intact, one sees what an intimate accessory the garden was, how it was almost drawn into the house, so to speak. The garden scheme is one of sequestered courts and open terraces. The villa is admirably set so as to have the advantage of every view, inwards or without. View it was that determined the placing of the long southern arcade looking to the main patio on one side and the distant Alhambra Palace on the other; also of the shorter arcade on the west overlooking the valley of the Darro River, and of the lofty loggias of the villa itself commanding the city.

So much for the scheme as considered from within; seen from a distance the placing is equally successful. Instead of crowning the hill, *El Cerro del Sol*, in the obvious manner, the architect set the villa well down the southern slope, thereby escaping north winds and giving it an air of basking comfortably in a well-cultivated expanse. The actual garden is seen to be concentrated within a walled enclosure for which the surrounding *huerta* makes a very decorative frame—the bright Indian-red earth kept plowed and friable, and dotted with myriad green tufts of orange and olive trees. When the former are heavy with fruit the hillside is like a rich woven fabric sparkling with threads of gold.

As the terracing walls of the *huerta* are untreated they do not conflict with those of the villa and garden; the eye goes immediately to the centre of the composition. Yet this focus modestly announces itself by nothing more than its shining white walls; there is no accentuated treatment leading up to it; no escalier and ramp, no balustraded terraces such as make up the impressive *partie* of the Italian villa. Rather in the medieval manner it leaves one to imagine where the approach is made. As a matter of fact, the original entrance was on the southwest or Alhambra side; but this was long ago abandoned in favour of the stately alley of cypresses that leads from the lodge towards, but not entirely to, the present highroad.

Of the porticoed villa which has stood dismantled for years there is not much to say; it is picturesque, not architectural. The most interesting feature about it is the disposition—master's quarters in one unit and this connected with the gate-lodge by two long shallow wings, one for service, the other a promenade. Thus the main patio is completely surrounded. The interior was never sumptuous, nothing more than cool white open loggias and rooms ornamented by carved yeseria or plasterwork which, if ever it was in polychrome, is now merely a deep ivory tone; nor are there any polychrome tiles. Marble was used for the columns of the delicate two-light (*ajimez*) windows and for the loggia arcades. On the walls are a few seventeenth-century imaginary portraits of its early Christian possessors, meaning the Moor aristocrat who married the Spanish *dame d'honneur*.

The principal garden is some hundred and fifty feet long, enclosed as described by buildings of several stories at each end (villa and gate-lodge respectively), and low ones along each side. That along the south is in the

BIRD'S EYE VIEW OF THE GENERALIFE, GRANADA

THE GENERALIFE SEEN FROM THE ALHAMBRA

LOOKING INTO THE ENTRANCE PATIO OF THE GENERALIFE FROM THE GATE-LODGE

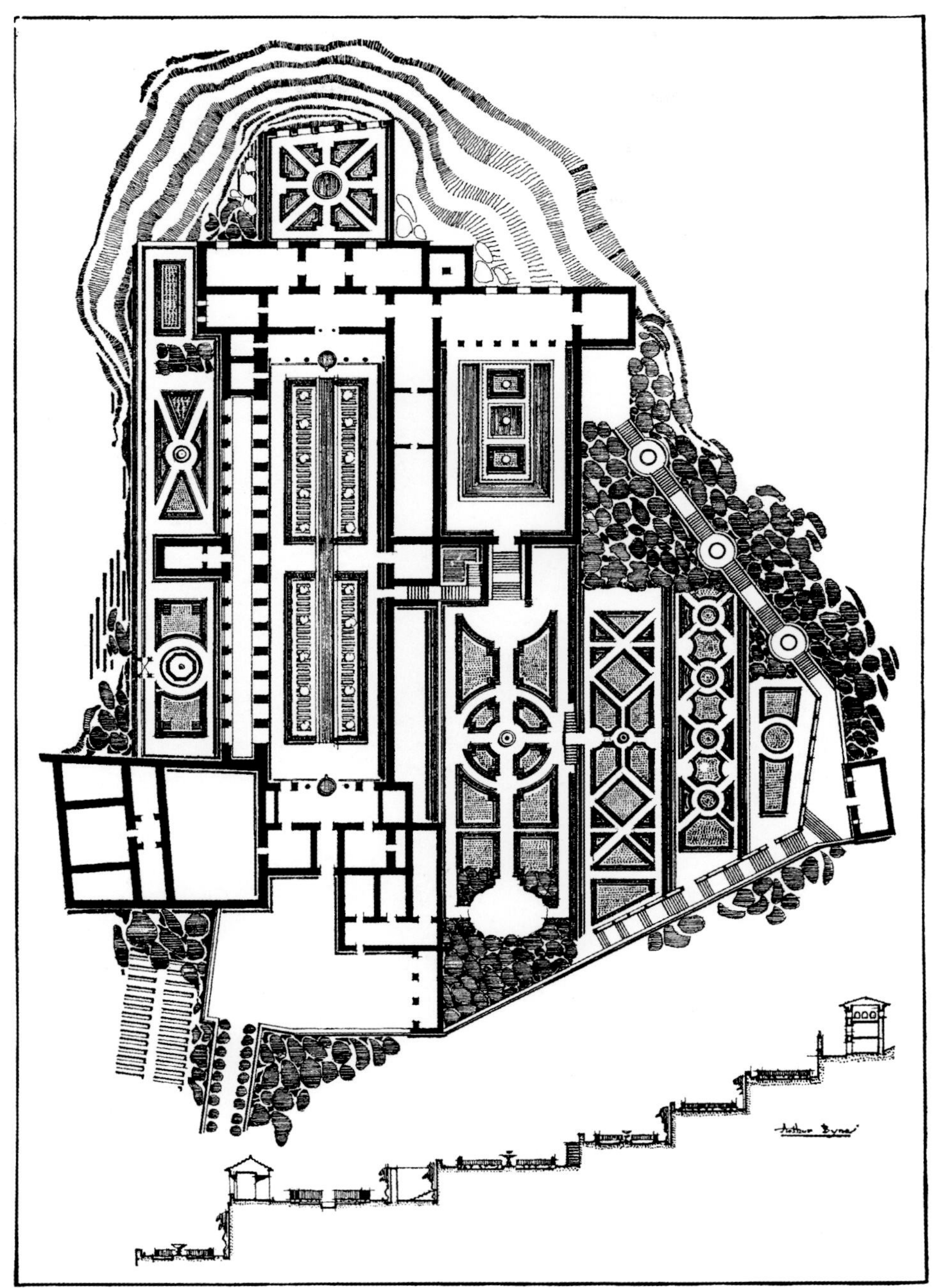

PLAN OF THE GENERALIFE, GRANADA

THE GENERALIFE GARDENS, PATIO OF THE CYPRESSES
Also called the water garden

THE GENERALIFE GARDENS. FOUNTAIN IN THE PATIO OF THE CYPRESSES

THE GENERALIFE GARDENS. LOGGIA IN WHITE STUCCO AND GREEN WOODWORK
Connecting the villa with the Cypress Patio

THE GENERALIFE GARDENS. THE PEBBLE WALK DESCENDING FROM THE HIGHEST TERRACE

THE GENERALIFE GARDENS. STAIR LEADING UP FROM THE CYPRESS PATIO
Landings laid in black and white river pebbles

THE GENERALIFE GARDENS. DETAIL OF STAIR
Leading from the Cypress Patio to the terrace above

THE GENERALIFE GARDENS. BRICK STAIR ASCENDING TO THE MIRADOR

form of an arcade interrupted midway by a diminutive mosque, now of course a chapel; corresponding on the north is a low service-wing. This last disguises an abrupt rise in the ground, its roof being just above the level of the upper garden. To run service-wings or other utilitarian structures along a terrace instead of building a lofty retaining wall was a practical solution. The idea is worth dwelling upon, though it is likely that a modern tenant of the villa (other than Spanish) would be more fastidious than the Moor about having his servants circulating freely through the main patio. The face of the service-wing is now all hidden, except for its green wooden doors, by neglected and unpruned growth of box and cypress.

Of the patio itself the chief *motif* is the canal that bisects it from end to end; not the typical narrow runlet of coloured tiles that one would find in Seville, but a serious three-foot marble *allée d'eau* through which a considerable volume of water is constantly flowing. The supply comes from several lively little mountain streams which were diverted from their course. Paths are of gravel; planting, now rather unkempt, is of low flowering herbs, the beds bordered by an ancient box hedge. In the way of accessories there is nothing but a shallow marble *tazza* at each end of the central canal and at each side the little spouts which send up thin jets of water to make a rainbow arch over its entire length.

Before entering the upper garden, which can be reached only through the villa, one should go downstairs and out into the attractive little formal garden at the rear with its hedges of box and arcaded wall opened to extend the garden view to the city. We shall see this same sort of wall very effectively borrowed in the new garden presently to be described, of Don José Acosta.

The upper court, named for the veteran cypresses which antedate the Christian conquest, is specially beautiful. From the villa it is reached by a few steps up into the portico which, set against a blank wall, forms its western boundary. The *Patio de los Cipreses* measures approximately twenty-five by eighty feet. It is in reality a water garden, but a Moorish water garden did not mean one broad sheet with aquatic plants and hydraulic curiosities, but merely an ample canal; embracing in this case three diminutive islands, its depth augmented by the reflection of the giant cypresses against the north wall. These, along with the hedges of myrtle and a few flowering shrubs on the islands, comprise the planting. A Renaissance marble fountain, jets of water edging the canals, coloured flower-pots, and the pebbled walks in black and white, compose the applied decoration. All here is green and green reflections; a spot where one can feel cool on even the hottest summer day.

The portico at the end, mentioned as giving access to the water garden, is balanced at the east by a stucco wall with an arched gateway. The wooden gate, like the doors of the portico, is painted green and opens upon the steps that rise to the next level. The landings are treated in elaborate pebble mosaics, and the stepped parapets at the sides hold potted flowers. Not until one has mounted to this third level is he free of the house and in the open garden; for the house acts as a connecting link between the two more intimate portions just described.

The third and succeeding levels are treated as open parterres, edged with box and myrtle and filled with chrysanthemums, roses, and lilies; the walls for the most part are concealed behind clipped and wired cypresses. In the centre of the parterre just entered, there used to stand a cypress arbour of eight trees domed in at the top, but it has been removed. Two distinct flights of steps lead up from the fourth level: that to the east is of brick and covered with a grape-arbour, that to the west is an amusing feature with circular landings and fountains at the various levels and with a grooved parapet lined with shallow roof tiles down which the water runs merrily. This whole *motif* is buried in a mass of thick foliage through which the sun's rays never penetrate and in which the stillness is only broken by the constant ripple of the water. A picturesque whitewashed mirador affording splendid views stands in the uppermost level, and the wall in front is surmounted by a row of busts in enamelled earthenware, probably of the seventeenth century and interesting as such.

As if to prove that tiles in colour were more Spanish than Moorish, this most Moorish of Andalusian gardens is at present devoid of them. It is quite probable however that the several mediocre fountains seen were built to replace ruinous ones of azulejos. Even were these restored one could still say that a charming garden had been created practically without the aid of tiled accessories; nor for that matter of any of the accessories that formed the usual stock-in-trade of the European garden-builder. In their place are simple stuccoed walls, coloured flower-pots, pebbled pavements, and sparkling water.

THE GENERALIFE. WINDOW WITH WOODEN GRILLE, OR REJA, IN THE GARDEN WALL

VI

THE ALHAMBRA, GRANADA
THE ACOSTA GARDEN, GRANADA

CHAPTER VI

THE ALHAMBRA, GRANADA
THE ACOSTA GARDEN, GRANADA

THE ALHAMBRA

THE Alhambra having been both fortress and palace, its gardens did not pass beyond the ramparts, but took the form of a series of patios within the palace precincts. It is, therefore, a hilltop, not a hillside, example—the acropolis levelled, and the sides of the mountain left wild and unterraced. The plan shows the same succession of rectangular units, some open to the sky, others ceiled, that made up the Moorish flat garden and palace. It is necessarily incomplete, for what is seen to-day is only a fraction of the original scheme.

Most of the vast royal residence that fell to the Catholic Sovereigns dated from the reigns of Yusuf I and Mohammed V—the fourteenth century. Ferdinand and Isabella gave orders for its restoration and upkeep; also they made a few alterations. Their grandson, Charles V, while he rebuked the canons of Córdova for tearing out the centre of the great mosque in order to install the Renaissance high altar and choir, did not hesitate to demolish a large part of the Alhambra group, structures and gardens, to make room for his never-to-be-completed Renaissance palace. His minor demolitions are less regrettable since he replaced them by something more harmonious than the Italian palace

—we refer to the series of rooms and patios which were prepared for his residence pending the new construction. With these intrusions the Alhambra gardens as they stand to-day are a combination of Moorish, early Spanish interpretation of Moorish, and Spanish Renaissance —this last in the *Jardin de los Adarves* (flat wall tops) which Charles V laid out down on the ramparts, to the left of the modern entrance. Most of their *cinquecento motifs* and sculpture have disappeared, but the box hedges and the rampart walls covered with vines seem to do quite well without them.

Dominating the plan is the long Moorish patio, one hundred and twenty feet by seventy-five—*El Patio de los Arrayanes* (myrtle) or, to give it its Arab name, *de la Alberca* (pool). First to be entered, it gives the impression of a golden glow everywhere, warm yellow arcaded walls, their reflection in the pool heightened by the myriads of goldfishes that dart about. Of planting, nothing more than the myrtle hedge; of embellishment, nothing but the marble pavement and the low basin at each end of the pool; this may sound *pauvre*, but it must be borne in mind that such walls would make, in themselves, any enclosure beautiful. Specially graceful are the arcades at each end, supported on slender marble colonnettes with delicate capitals, that to the south surmounted by a beautiful little triforium gallery.

The only other large patio left is that of the *Leones* on opposite axis to that just described. It was laid out in 1377, and measures ninety-two feet by fifty-two. Its

THE ALHAMBRA PARK OR ALAMEDA, GRANADA, FOUNTAIN OF CHARLES V
Designed by the Italian-trained architect, Machuca

THE ALHAMBRA PALACE AND GARDENS. FOUNTAIN IN THE PATIO DE DARAXA
Faceted Moorish tazza and Renaissance lower basin

THE ALHAMBRA. FOUNTAIN IN THE COURT OR PATIO LOS LEONES

THE ALHAMBRA. UPPER GALLERY
Commanding a little garden on one side and the city on the other

THE ALHAMBRA. LOWER ENTRANCE TO THE PATIO DE LA REJA, (OR OF JOAN THE MAD)
Typical wooden spindle doors

THE ALHAMBRA. PAVEMENT OF THE PATIO DE LA REJA SEEN FROM AN UPPER GALLERY

THE ALHAMBRA, LOOKING FROM THE PATIO DE LA REJA INTO THE PATIO DE DARAXA

THE ALHAMBRA. UPPER AND LOWER GALLERIES ALONG THE NORTH SIDE OF THE PATIO DE LA REJA

CAMPO DE LOS MARTIRES, GRANADA
A series of walled terraces

planting, said to have been all of dwarf orange-trees, has disappeared—nothing but gravel takes its place. As far as the garden part is concerned only the famous—the over-famous—fountain remains, along with eight shallow basins at the ends, connected by little canals with the central overflow. The Fountain of Lions, standing out as it now does without the kindly proximity of trees or shrubs, does not seem to merit the praise generally bestowed upon it. The noble beast is conventionalized even beyond heraldic recognition, and the spout protruding from his mouth hardly adds dignity. More admirable is the basin the lions support, mellowed into most beautiful colour. All four sides of this patio are arcaded, making a splendid display of slender marble columns and capitals. At each end is a pavilion with a wooden dome of typical Moorish carpentry.

The two patios just described are the most genuinely oriental of the Alhambra; beautiful though they are in their way, it is rather the smaller Christian (by way of apposition) enclosures that offer the modern garden-builder greater inspiration. Among these, either remodelled or created by the destruction of Moorish portions, are the *Patio de Daraxa* and the *Patio de la Reja*, which deserve special attention. In the former, dating from the time of Charles V, is a beautiful stone fountain, consisting of an upper Moorish basin brought from the Mexuar Patio and mounted on a Renaissance base. Here we see the ancient practice of scoring and faceting the edges and under side of the upper basin so that the thousand little high lights thus created may be reflected and magnified in the pool below. Planting is entirely green—clipped box and cypress trees. Washington Irving, who had lodgings in the abandoned Alhambra, was specially fond of this spot. "Here," he wrote, "the twittering martlet, the only bird sacred and unmolested in Spain because it is believed to have plucked the thorns from Our Saviour's crown as He hung on the cross, builds his nest and breaks the silence of these sequestered courts which were made for oriental enjoyment."

The other patio buried in the heart of the building is that of the Reja, on the north side; very diminutive, built in 1654. Its name refers to a window grille through which the imprisoned Jane the Mad (*Juana la Loca*) is said to have looked out during her enforced residence in the Alhambra. The pavement of patterned stone is specially beautiful. In the corners are circles of earth from which rise lofty cypresses; additional green is supplied by potted bamboo plants. Off to one side and thus placed in order to be visible from the adjacent patios, is the marble fountain. Further interest is supplied by the wooden spindled gates which connect with the ground-floor chambers of the palace. These gates are a very Spanish feature—an economical interpretation of forged iron and found in gardens and in the poorer churches. Enclosing the north side of this little patio and at second-story level is an open gallery commanding a sweeping view over the Albaicin Hill. For its construction, Moorish columns and capitals were brought from demolished courts. Spaniards never missed an opportunity for introducing this sort of promenade gallery, attractive in itself and open to both the garden and the distant landscape.

Of the Alhambra palace we say nothing. As a Moorish monument in a European country it is interesting and even beautiful, but the majority of Europeans (we use the word in reference to race as opposed to Asiatics) feel no sympathy with the much cusped arches, the never-ending wainscots of polychrome tile all in the prescribed Mohammedan patterns of interlacings and arabesques, and the highly coloured plasterwork of the walls repeating these same interminable geometric designs. Somehow it does not appeal to our more sober northern taste. Its ready adaptability to café and dance-hall decoration puts us who are essentially domestic by instinct out of sorts with it. It represents the artistic decadence of the race that built it. Had the Christian régime in Córdova and Seville, which were won two and a half centuries before Granada, left us a single untampered-with relic of the earlier Moorish period when azulejos were used with restraint and yesería was probably not painted at all, we might feel more in harmony with it.

THE GARDEN OF DON JOSÉ ACOSTA

We are fortunate in being able to illustrate one new Granada garden, not only for its beauty but also because it shows how happily the old Andalusian type may be combined with certain features of European gardens in general. It is the creation of the painter, Don José Rodriguez Acosta. Admiration of antique sculpture has led Señor Acosta to study how it could best be introduced into the typical local setting. He chose his site on the precipitous southern slope of the Monte Mauror, close to the Alhambra. This was the ancient *Campo de los Martires*, legend making it the scene of early Christian persecutions, and later, of the dungeons where were thrown at night the Christian captives who worked on the Alhambra.

Structurally the garden is Andalusian. Great stepped retaining walls follow down the hillside, garden courts are enclosed by arcaded walls similar to those already described in the Generalife, and parts of the garden lie in the embrace of the house itself, as at the Alhambra; but all this is much more achitectural than in the prototypes, displaying, indeed, an extraordinary appreciation of ancient Roman building principles. Andalusian tradition is departed from by the introduction of garden sculpture, a columnar exedra, and a general use of the orders. There are no polychrome tiles, and in truth their introduction would seem trivial in the monumental scale of things. The planting is wholly green, cypress and box. Water is not running and rippling in the more Spanish fashion, but lies in quiet pools, and the only colour these reflect besides white and green is the deep blue of the southern sky. As this garden is still unfinished it is somewhat unfair to the owner to illustrate it; at the same time it is too promising and too inspiring to be omitted.

Further along this same southern slope is a villa or *Carmen* with a fine terraced garden, known as the *Carmen de los Martires*. It is a mid-Victorian interpretation of Andalusian, most interesting for its orange terraces and the use of potted plants along the parapets. In recent years it has become quite overgrown and formless, but many beautiful little spots can still be found.

THE MASSIVE WALL ENCLOSING THE GARDEN OF DON JOSÉ ACOSTA ON THE SLOPES OF MONTE MAUROR, GRANADA

View from the road

THE ARCADED WALL OF THE ACOSTA GARDEN SEEN FROM THE ROAD

THE ACOSTA GARDEN DEPARTS FROM THE ANDALUSIAN TRADITION BY INTRODUCING CLASSIC ACCESSORIES

THE ACOSTA GARDEN. TEMPLE AND ARCHWAY OVERLOOKING GRANADA

THE ACOSTA GARDEN. THE STEPPED WALL AND THE SIERRA NEVADA BEYOND

POOL IN THE ACOSTA GARDEN
The lofty wall is perforated by arches to diminish the heaviness

THE ACOSTA GARDEN, A STUDY IN RETAINING WALLS

VII

THE ALCAZAR GARDENS, SEVILLE

ENTRANCE TO THE ALCAZAR GARDENS WITH AN OVER-
PORTAL IN BLUE AND YELLOW TERRA COTTA

CHAPTER VII

THE ALCAZAR GARDENS, SEVILLE

SEVILLE offers, in the park of its *Alcazar*, the most complete early Spanish example of the level type. In addition the city contains the gardens of the Alba and Medinaceli palaces and the modern *Parque de Maria Luisa;* while in the way of very small gardens and patios there are any number that will amply reward the searcher who is bold enough to bribe his way into them.

From classic times the site of the Alcazar has been important in the history of Seville. After the Romans, the Moors built their citadel (Arab, *al-Kasr*) here; this was towards the end of the twelfth century, Seville's most prosperous Moorish period. Of this building nothing remains. Its precincts were vast, having extended down to the Guadalquivir and included the ground now occupied by the *Fabrica de Tabacos*, the *Palacio Santelmo*, and the *Torre del Oro*. For the rebuilding of the destroyed Alcazar Peter the Cruel (1350-69) deserves the credit. As his architects and craftsmen were Moors and as the palace is proof that they were following their own oriental tradition in architecture, we may safely presume that the garden they made for him was also after their own manner.

How much of their layout was preserved by Christian monarchs can never be more than a matter of conjecture.

Charles V meddled with both palace and garden; considering that practically all the tiles seen in the latter date from the sixteenth century and onwards, one would not be far wrong in assuming that Peter the Cruel's had less of them and was thus truer to precedent. Within the palace, however, and dating from his time are fine early examples—cuerda secas, cuencas, and even mosaics—which those who are interested in old tiles should not fail to examine. The garden was again remodelled but only in part by Philip IV and Philip V. The latter is said to have added a fish-pool; if this means the main pool on the uppermost level it is likely that it was on the site of a former reservoir, for from this point the whole garden is, and apparently always was, irrigated.

As to scheme, it is chiefly absent. The layout is made up of the usual series of walled enclosures falling haphazardly in line. Even with so much ground at their command the gardeners never thought of creating long vistas nor planting alleys of trees. The main point to observe in the plan is that the enclosures nearest the palace are smallest, averaging seventy-five by a hundred feet, and admitting of more intimate treatment; while in the larger ones the set-out plot units remain much the same, but are repeated in order to fill a given area and thus keep all in the same scale. Where the plan shows, as it does on its outer edge, greater motivation, even the layman's eye will instantly detect the eighteenth century. Of the vapidity of those decadent "Philippine days" nothing could speak more eloquently than the ambitious but fortunately unfinished project in the northwest corner beyond the courts of Maria Padilla.

The Alcazar grounds are entered at the uppermost level, which brings one immediately to the main irrigation pool, backed up by the rococo wall or rather, rococo facing to Peter the Cruel's fortified wall. From this eminence one descends at once to the main level. The first parterre parallel to the palace is known as the *Jardines de Maria Padilla*. Opening on this are the several vaulted grottos where, if legend be true, this mistress of Peter the Cruel used to bathe. The paths of contrary axes lead to the so-called baths of Jane the Mad and the pavilion which her son Charles V built. The Padilla parterre and the plaisance of Charles V are, to our mind, the best of the Alcazar Gardens.

These gardens, being fairly large, offer a special chance to appreciate the effectiveness of long stretches of pleached white walls. Those contiguous to the palace extend up to the second-story terraces, and their tops are turned into promenades and provided with a continuous parapet seat. Thus the inmates might step out and walk through the garden at second-story level, so to speak. Where walls of different height abut, the two levels are connected by parapeted steps. The top of the north or fortified and buttressed wall is likewise connected with the palace terrace by means of an arched passage over the entrance to the gardens; while the arcaded gallery built in the thickness of the wall can be reached either by a stair from the garden or a passage from the palace. Facing south, as it does, this wall gallery is sheltered from cold winds in winter and hot sun in summer — a practical as well as a decorative feature. Although none of the garden walls have fine iron or wooden gates there are several recessed window openings, treated in tile, that are particularly beautiful.

The only decorative accessory is the azulejo. Indeed, these gardens are a veritable museum of fine mellowed sixteenth-century azulejos; yet for all their prodigality there is a restraint as compared with the new Sevillian work. This is particularly noticeable in the pavements, mostly in unglazed dark red without coloured insets. On the other hand fountains, basins, benches, stairs, and the Emperor's pavilion, are all in polychrome. Best among the fountains are those at the intersections of paths—low, star-shaped, and treated in yellows, greens, and blues. These appear to have been taken as the model for every new fountain placed in Seville in the last ten years.

The polychrome bench is here seen at its best because, being of considerable length, it has not the abruptness of the short park bench of three or four seats. In combination with walls that measure from fifty to seventy feet long, or set against an equally long hedge, it almost achieves monumentality. Near the pavilion so often referred to is a *rond pont* featured with a circular bench in four sections, which is particularly interesting for its colour. Unbacked, the bench is set against a high mass of box, with whose deep green the brilliant yellow, blue, and light green sixteenth-century pisanos make delight-

Photo Lacoste

GENERAL VIEW OF THE ALCAZAR GARDENS, SEVILLE, SHOWING THE WALL PROMENADES

Photo Lacoste
GENERAL VIEW OF THE ALCAZAR GARDENS TAKEN TWENTY-FIVE YEARS AGO BEFORE NEW TREES WERE PLANTED

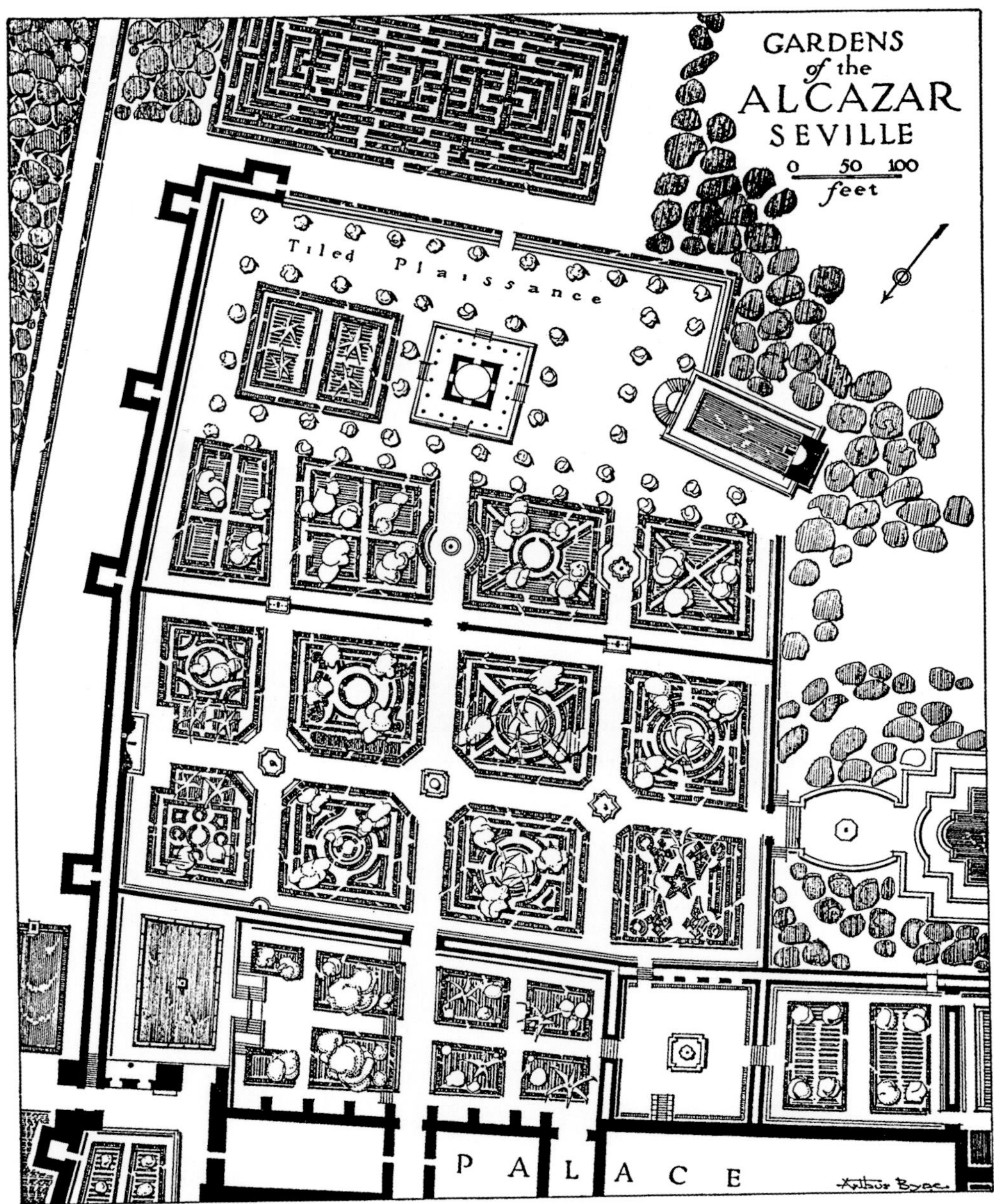

PLAN OF THE ALCAZAR GARDENS
Double walls indicate a promenade on top

THE ALCAZAR GARDENS. POOL AND ENTRANCE LOGGIA

THE ALCAZAR. A PAVED PATIO BETWEEN TWO PLANTED PLOTS

THE ALCAZAR. GARDEN OF MARIA PADILLA, ADJACENT TO THE PALACE

THE ALCAZAR GARDENS. PLANTING FORMS A GREEN BACKGROUND FOR THE POLYCHROME TILE ACCESSORIES

THE ALCAZAR GARDENS. DIFFERENCES OF LEVEL HAVE BEEN PURPOSELY CREATED TO ADD INTEREST

THE ALCAZAR GARDENS. THE WALLED ENCLOSURES ARE CONNECTED BY GRILLED OPENINGS

THE ALCAZAR. GALLERY IN THE THICKNESS OF PETER THE CRUEL'S WALL
A sheltered promenade overlooking the gardens

THE ALCAZAR GARDENS. PAVILION OF CHARLES V
The coloured tiles are among the finest in Seville

THE ALCAZAR GARDENS. BAROQUE PAVILION AND THE SO-CALLED POOL OF JOAN THE MAD

ful harmony. The French gardener who arranged the Ronda place already illustrated did something of the same sort with very good results.

As a tile creation the Emperor's summer house and the court in which it stands are a *chef-d'œuvre*. The former we have described, calling attention to the fine lustre tiles, of which not many remain to-day in Seville. It is set in the centre of the court covering about half an acre, and this whole space is paved with unglazed red tiles laid in herring-bone. Innumerable little circular beds for orange trees are edged with coloured tiles, and around the enclosing wall runs a continuous tile bench. The trees, well clipped into spherical form and neatly set in their round earth pockets, appear dwarfed, as if they belonged to an embroidery or tapestry. When thick with fruit nothing could be more decorative than the golden green spotting in conjunction with the coloured tiles. As a garden this spot has somewhat the quality of a primitive painting—perhaps for the same reason: it has *no drawing*, all is off axis and askew for no apparent reason, yet the result is charm.

Commenting on the plan of the Alcazar gardens it was observed that the walled enclosures nearest the palace (*de Maria Padilla*) were smaller and treated more intimately; meaning that they were more like outdoor rooms. As an extension of the living apartments they were kept very formal, mostly in tiles. Practically the only planting is against the white walls, which are made beautiful by vines and pleached trees.

The only bloom is that provided by potted plants set freely about (*en passant*, the large pots of cream glaze with the royal arms in blue are commendably unpretentious and do not try to rival the polychrome of the tiles). The first section, practically flowerless except when its immense and very impressive oleander tree is in bloom, offers an enchanting play of soft colour as one enters from the upper level—glossy, purplish green in the oleander leaves, waxy yellowish green in the lemon trees, and all the shades between; brilliant yellow and blue in the tiled fountains and benches, and their reflections in the broad basin heightened by the potted carnations that stand around. Out of these simple elements plus a few lordly peacocks a masterpiece of colouring has been created.

A great deal of interest is added to these courts by their being at slightly different level and connected by tiled stairs. The whole garden terrain was probably equally flat, and these differences were intentionally created. Another effective detail that deserves mention and which we also suspect to have been intentional is the slight deflection of the main axis; by this trick, in the long vista through the several patios one always gets one side of the arched reveal beyond instead of merely the blank opening.

In the next and much larger parterre parallel to the Padilla, planting is the main feature; eight big plots set out in mazes of box and myrtle. These mazes are of every conceivable design, geometric and scroll. Here are found the previously mentioned insignia of the military orders outlined in box. Above these densely planted beds rise lofty date-palms—the whole forming a green shade garden.

A more attractive garden than this of the Alcazar is hard to imagine. Wandering through it one feels the childish simplicity of the plan and is convinced that it must date back at least to Peter the Cruel's reign, if not earlier. Charles V's half-trained Spanish Italianists, had they started with virgin soil, would have attempted an ambitious *partie* and felt it necessary to dissimulate the irregularities of the site by some recognized academic solution. Confronted by an existing Moorish layout, they wisely took the line of least resistance and did but little to modify it. Philip IV and Philip V's gardeners were less prudent; their trivial rococo revetment, *à la Boboli*, to the sturdy old medieval wall and their effort to *Louisize* the garden area to the west are distinctly unpleasant anomalies.

GARDENS OF THE ALCAZAR. STAIR OF POLYCHROME TILES BUILT IN THE THICKNESS OF THE WALL AND LEADING TO A PROMENADE GALLERY ON TOP

VIII

GARDEN OF THE DUKE OF MEDINACELI, SEVILLE
GARDEN OF THE DUKE OF ALVA, SEVILLE

CHAPTER VIII

GARDEN OF THE DUKE OF MEDINACELI, SEVILLE
GARDEN OF THE DUKE OF ALVA, SEVILLE

THE two most important old Sevillian palaces with gardens are known popularly as the *Casa de Pilatos* and the *Casa de las Dueñas.* The first belongs to the Duke of Medinaceli, the second to the Duke of Alva; two ancient titles by the way, which head the list of Spanish nobility.

Intermarriage of these two ducal houses with the powerful Ribera family of Seville explains the present ownership. In the late fourteenth century the Riberas, who lived in princely style, bought the Dueñas mansion, its owner having to sell it in order to ransom his son from the Moors of Granada. The new owners continued the building on a magnificent scale and at the same time built the Pilatos Palace, which was supposed by Sevillians of the period to be a copy of that once occupied by the Roman governor of Judea. It is the garden of this latter that first claims attention.

If built in any other country in the sixteenth century both houses would have been in the Renaissance style and accompanied by Italian gardens. In Seville, where architects and gardeners were Moors, all is a mingling of Moorish and Christian elements. In each case the palace plan is the usual grouping of rectangles around open patios, and the embellishment, except for a few marble details, is in azulejos, yesería, and Moorish carpentry in the form of artesonados and panelled doors and shutters. The Renaissance marble entrance to the Pilatos was ordered from representatives in Seville of the Genoese marble *ateliers* and shipped from Genoa, along with the famous Ribera tombs, to the city on the Guadalquivir; but it is significant that the shipment did not include the characteristic Italian garden embellishments of the day. The main patio of the Pilatos house has no planting, for which reason it is less attractive than that of the Dueñas; on the other hand, the gardens surrounding the house are finer.

THE MEDINACELI GARDEN

The gardens, representing but a fraction of the original grounds (which suffered bombardment in the uprising of 1840), consist of two distinct parts, the tiled to the southeast and the green to the northwest. The former is distinctly Andalusian, the latter European in a nondescript but very agreeable way. The Andalusian might be described as a Spanish triumph in back-yard treatment, for the space devoted to it abuts on the rear of a street of humble dwellings. It is surrounded by an exclusion wall, all white like the house; this averages twenty feet in height, leaving little more than the picturesque rooftops of the neighbourhood visible. (Madrid might learn a useful lesson here; hardly a palace in the capital but has sixty-foot "spite walls" on one side at least of its grounds, which, even could they be made things of beauty *per se*, would rob any garden of scale.) The Sevillian wall in question is surmounted by a cresting and is screened by bougainvillea and black-stemmed bamboo, always particularly decorative against white. The tiled garden at its base is divided into five panels, three of planting, one wholly of tiles, and one given over to the pool (*estanque*). Little attempt was made by the designer to compose them either in relation to each other or to the house. Rather they appear to have been laid out much as one would spread fine old rugs on a floor of irregular perimeter, without the least concern over the resulting discrepancies.

To simplify description these panels have been lettered on the plan.

Panel A is a study in limited planting and coloured earths—eight garden-plots on a court of brilliant yellow clay. Around each plot is a double curb, blue tile and brick, and between the two, deep reddish earth sparsely planted with freesia. Set inside of this further to define the centre is an edging of green wooden hoops on whose outer side are planted little toylike clumps of myrtle kept down to six inches. The centre itself, of rich black earth, contains a variety of shrubs and flowers, among the latter violets, begonias, and sweet lavender ; in the corners of each bed and not visible in our photographs of three years ago, are large rounded shrubs. There is no tile fountain or basin; the only feature introduced by way of adornment is the statue at the far end against the vine-covered wall. This is one of the large collection of Roman antiques brought back in the latter part of the sixteenth century by Per Afan de Ribera, Viceroy of Naples.

Panel B is wholly taken up by the pool. Some twenty by thirty-eight feet, it is built of cement with a rounded coping. At the wall end is a fragment of sculpture and the water surface is largely covered with large, flat lily leaves. Dark ivy and brilliant nasturtiums outline the whole pool.

In Panel C we have a tiled garden at its best. The entire area is paved, permitting no other planting than that of a small date-palm in each corner. Flat red tiles laid basket-weave with coloured insets were used for the pavement. Built-in features consist of the flat central fountain, the tiled bench along the pool-side, and opposite, the white retaining wall edged with green tile, of the corner panel which lies four feet higher. In this wall and on axis with the fountain is the double flight of steps leading up. To emphasize the artificiality of this panel, there is no planting against either the low retaining wall nor the high enclosing wall at the back. The pavement is frequently wet down during the day and glistens like a jewel. "Smart" in its most modish sense is the only suitable adjective thoroughly to describe this area.

Panels D and E are laid out with yellow clay paths and trim garden-plots edged with blue and white tiles. Ground ivy and myrtle make the borders, and the centre is densely planted with herbaceous shrubs. The few Roman and Moorish columns placed about blend harmoniously.

This is a precious bit of Andalusian gardening, and

for its restoration the *Duque de Medinaceli* and his architects are to be congratulated; also for rescuing from threatened ruin the beautiful Renaissance iron reja which used to guard a window in a small and obscure rear patio and has now been brought out to a position more worthy of it, facing panel A.

The green garden to the northwest of the house is also to be admired, but is far less striking than the one just described. Like the loggias of the palace which so agreeably face on its several axes, the arrangement of the plan reflects Italian influence; in the details of planting and paths, however, we see the local tradition. The tiled paths are set almost a foot above the general level to permit of irrigation; and with this same end in view the earth is banked in patterns like miniature labyrinths. With the planting practically limited to deciduous shrubs and trees the garden has a quite European look.

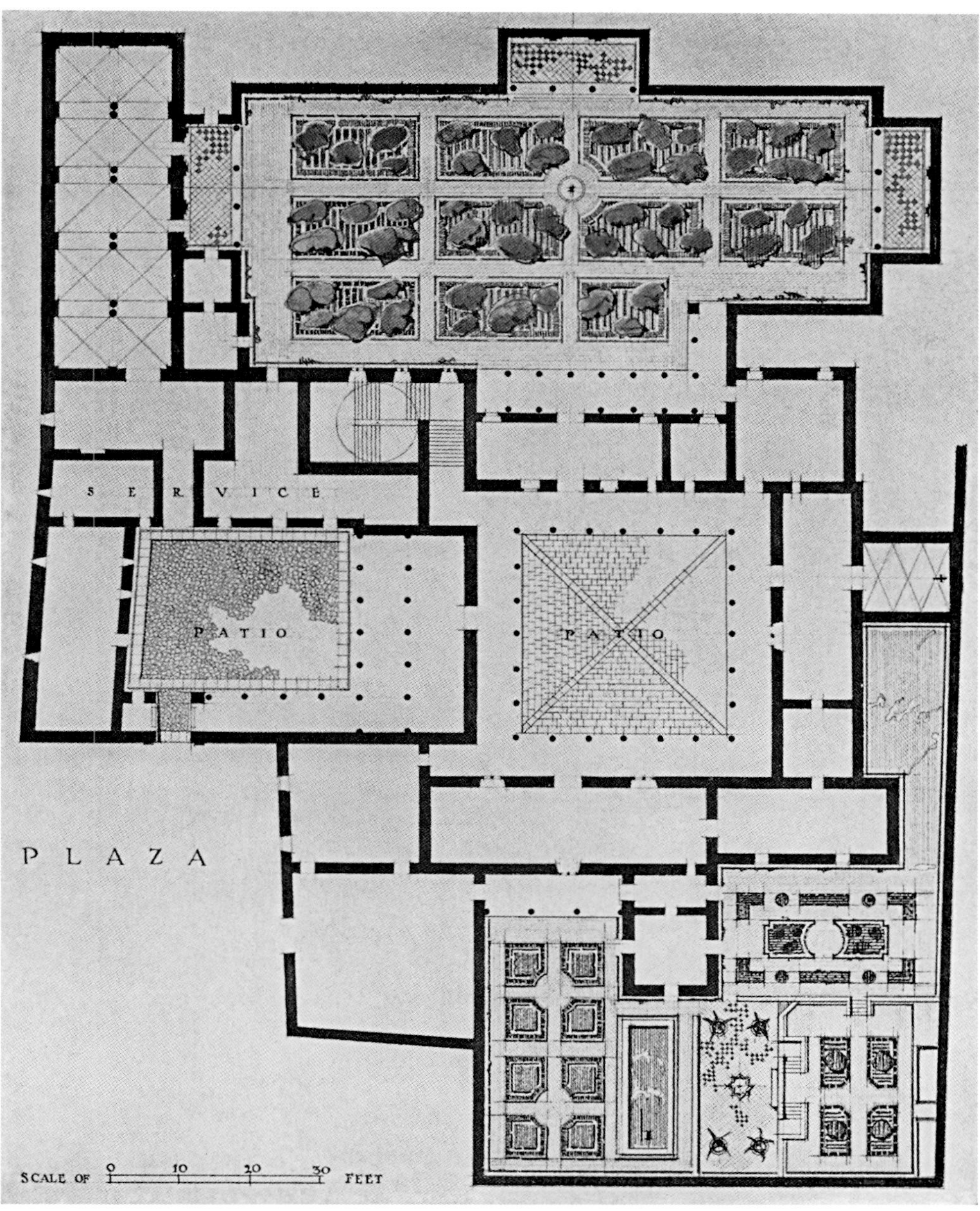

PLAN OF THE DUKE OF MEDINACELI'S PALACE AND GARDEN, SEVILLE

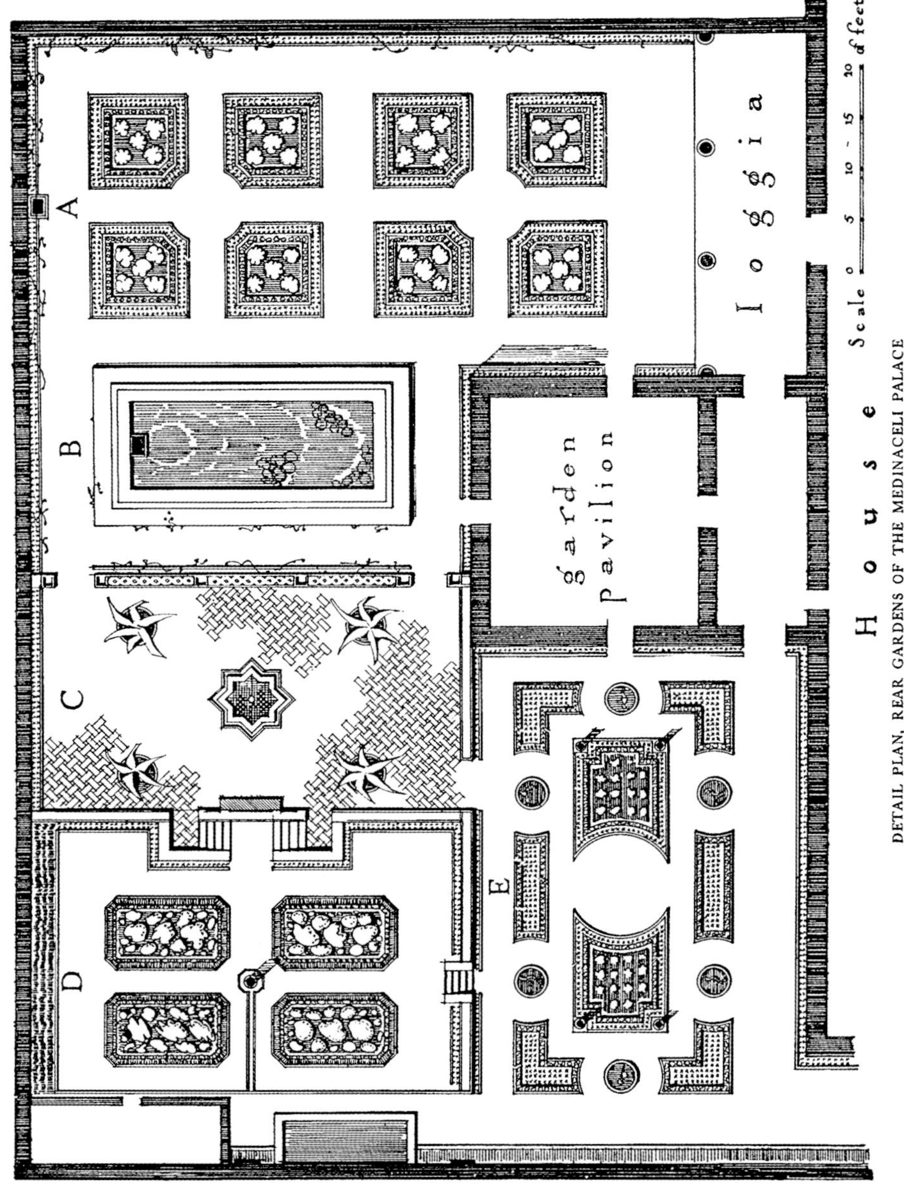

DETAIL PLAN, REAR GARDENS OF THE MEDINACELI PALACE
Showing plots A, B, C, D and E

GARDEN OF THE MEDINACELI PALACE. PLOT A
Paths of tamped yellow clay and beds of black loam edged with coloured tiles

THE MEDINACELI GARDEN. PLOT B
A long narrow pool edged with ivy and nasturtiums

THE MEDINACELI GARDEN. PLOTS C AND D
Excellent examples of the Sevillian tiled treatment

THE MEDINACELI GARDEN. DETAILS OF PLOT C

Polychrome tile

THE MEDINACELI GARDEN. PLOT E
A clay court set out with beds of close-clipped planting to simulate grass

THE MEDINACELI GARDEN. PLOT E
A combination of free planting and tile accessories

GARDEN OF THE DUKE OF ALVA

The Alva palace is usually referred to by the name of the small street, *Calle de las Dueñas*, from which it is entered. According to records it was once of much greater extent and contained no less than sixteen patios. Now it has but two. Perhaps, like the Pilatos palace, some of it was demolished during the uprising against Isabel II, and the large forecourt, so rare in Spain, where palaces were placed flush with the street, may once have been occupied or enclosed by buildings. Neither forecourt nor façade is specially interesting; in Moorish fashion the attractions are reserved for the interior patios and the gardens behind.

As seen in the plan, the forecourt is laid out in a planted oval bisected by a straightaway. Around the sides and banked thick against the walls are pepper trees, lantana, acacia, and Spanish gorse. Against the house-wall, to the right on entering, is a fine tiled watering-trough, an old-time necessity which in Spain has not yet given place to the gasoline pump.

Passing through the sanded *zaguan* or outer vestibule the principal patio is entered. This is Moorish in full decadence, rich and luxurious; a little museum of all that Moorish artisans were producing in the sixteenth century for Christian masters and hence classified like the Pilatos patio as *Mudejar*—carved plasterwork, wooden ceilings, and azulejos. As to this last item, those who are interested in Moorish lustre can see in the family chapel to the left of the patio the finest tiles with gold reflections (*reflejos metalicos*) left in Spain. The patio garden is simple in contrast to the architecture. Paths are placed on the diagonal, thus not calling attention to the fact that the entrance is off centre; at their intersection is a built-up basin of coloured tiles around a marble fountain. Originally the paths were laid in mosaic of polychrome marbles. When it became necessary to repave, unglazed brick was used, but a few panels of the mosaic were saved. As seen in the bird's-eye view, planting is reduced to a minimum. Beds are of black earth and outlined by dwarf box. Ancient date-palms tower high overhead, at their base a circle or star-form planted in lilies. The intervening area is neatly dotted with little tufts of dwarf juniper. All is set out and kept up with great precision. Lining the parapet of the patio are hundreds of flower-pots, whose contents vary with the season; in either carnation or chrysanthemum time they form a veritable cresting of brilliant bloom to the wall.

A minor patio off to the left has never been refurbished and is none the less attractive for that reason. Surrounded by a plain brick pavement is a mellowed old basin built up of emerald green and purple tiles. This colouring along with that of the raised violet beds is in delightful contrast to the immaculate walls.

To the right of the entrance-patio is a typical Spanish screen-wall separating the house from the grounds. Through its several grilled openings nice perspectives may be obtained of the garden beyond. This is quite informal and consists of four main plots with the usual fountain in the centre. The beds, outlined with hedges and shaded by lofty palms, supply the cut flowers for the house. Passing around the staircase wing and by the pool, one enters the irregular garden precinct at the rear. Here planting consists almost exclusively of orange trees, and to permit of their constant irrigation, the paths are raised high above the level of the ground. Along the walls of the house are pleached geraniums growing to a height of twenty feet. Azulejos are conspicuous by their absence, and the whole effect is that of a rustic grove rather than of a city garden.

In examining an Andalusian plan it must be remembered that the house is divided horizontally into summer and winter quarters. Into the lower or summer story very little outside light and no sun are allowed to enter. Nearly all the openings give onto the patio, whose planting and fountain help to cool the air. The lower rooms themselves often have floor fountains whose open conduit leads out to the patio basin. In the case of the Dueñas plan the large dining-hall across the back has the benefit of both the patio and the garden, one end, that towards the pool, having been left open in the form of a loggia.

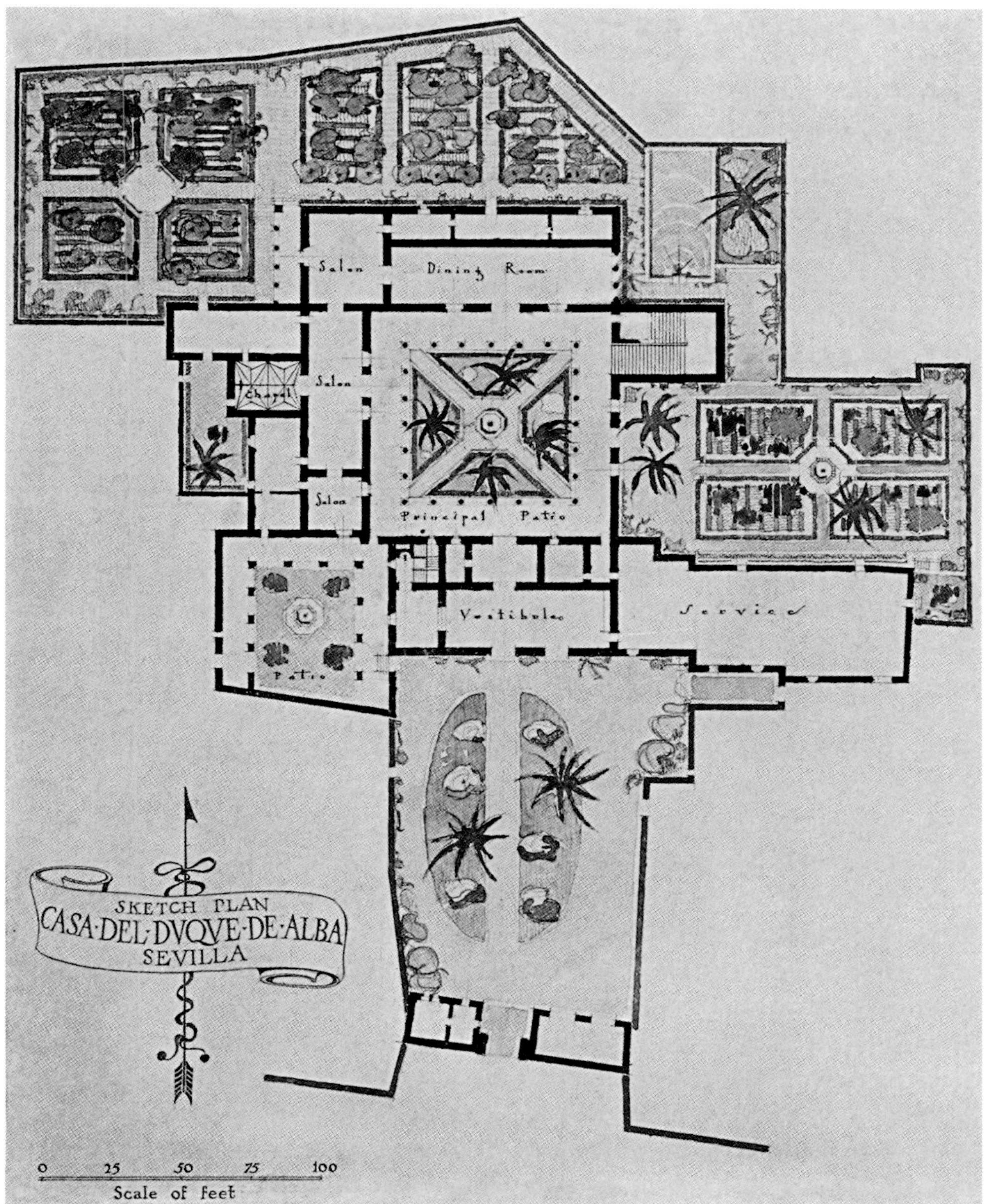

PLAN OF THE CASA DE DUQUE DE ALVA, SEVILLE
From "Spanish Architecture of the Sixteenth Century". Permission of the Hispanic Society of America

FRONT GARDEN OF THE ALVA PALACE
Watering trough of polychrome tile

PRINCIPAL PATIO OF THE ALVA PALACE
Diagonal paths divide the court into four plots outlined with dwarf box

THE ALVA PATIO, WITH IRON GRILLES TOWARDS THE GARDEN

GALLERY OVERLOOKING THE ALVA PATIO
The whole parapet is set out with potted plants

A MINOR PATIO IN THE ALVA PALACE
Planted with bougainvillea and violets

THE ALVA PATIO SEEN FROM THE GALLERY
Grass being difficult to grow, the plots are dotted with diminutive clumps like "hen and chickens"

IX

SOME GARDENS OF SEVILLE AND CORDOVA

CONVENTO DE LA MERCED
SEVILLA
BYNE

CHAPTER IX

SOME GARDENS OF SEVILLE AND CORDOVA

PARQUE DE MARIA LUISA, SEVILLE

THE modern *Parque de Maria Luisa* has recently been prepared for the *mise en scène* of the Spanish-American Exposition. The whole extensive area known by this name was once the garden of the Duc de Montpensier, brother-in-law to Isabel II, and surrounded the great Baroque palace of Santelmo. Towards the end of the last century his widow, Maria Luisa, presented the palace and the grounds nearest to it to the Archbishopric of Seville, and the remoter and larger portion of her nondescript park to the public. This was known as the Park of Maria Luisa. When Seville decided to arrange a Spanish-American Exposition the upper part of this park was chosen as the site. Building and garden-making were at once begun, but the Great War appears to have deterred indefinitely the opening of the exposition. All the preparations are in true Andalusian character; and if one feels that the buildings are perhaps too intensely regional, not so the gardens.

In these, as said, a Frenchman, M. Forrestier, collaborated. The same expert is now busy metamorphosing the once barren side of the Montjuich, Barcelona, into a public garden of great distinction. The problem at Seville was to lay out in the Andalusian manner an area vaster than any existing prototype; also to make it public in character and provide it with long drives and esplanades; yet to conform more or less to the previous layout, thus avoiding the expense of unmaking the old before starting the new. The solution is most creditable. The designers have given Seville what it never possessed before—a truly Andalusian public garden, enjoyed by all classes (who here know how to be happy in a park without bandstands, merry-go-rounds, cages of unfortunate wild beasts, soda-water fountains, and other embellishments which in certain countries are considered indispensable to mass recreation).

Although the Andalusian garden is usually without architectural features, one such indulgence—the pergola—was permitted here. Used sparingly without orders, it is merely a succession of square pillars surmounted by equally simple wooden beams. In every alternate bay are stucco benches, and their edging of green tiles and the lozenge-shape tile insert in each face of the pillar are the only decoration. The vines at the base of the uprights are interestingly confined in a trefoil formed by three common roof-tiles imbedded vertically. Another departure from precedent is the large *estanque*, perfectly rectangular and with an island of the same shape in the centre. Both borders of the water are accentuated by a stout brick coping, that of the island holding an unbroken row, hundreds and hundreds, of potted plants. The surface of the water is covered with lilies and frogbit. While this pool is larger than any other in Andalusia there is no doubt that it was suggested by the little water garden, or Court of the Cypresses, at the Generalife, whose rectangular simplicity and rows of flower-pots it repeats.

The tile fountains in the park are for the most part well designed, low and broad (as much cannot be said for the marble Fountain of the Lions—poorly carved, and the beast too realistic). Some of the polychromy is too garish, but in this matter it is probable that the over-enthusiastic tile-manufacturers of Triana had their say. A tile innovation that attracts, and justly, much attention is the outdoor reading-room. Not so much for its design, which happens to be excellent, but for its purpose. An exedra, to the memory of Cervantes, who spent weary months in a Sevillian prison, it tells the adventures of his fantastic hero, Don Quixote, in a fine series of burnt-clay pictures, while at each side of the seat is a tile book-stand where repose vellum-covered volumes of the great novelist. These for the mental refreshment of the loiterer; and not chained like the old-fashioned park tin cup, but at the disposition of all—richman, poorman, beggarman, even thief. This charming and respected corner makes our own park nooks, all too often bestrewn with hideous comic picture supplements and the other débris of "nature-lovers," exceedingly sad by contrast.

Worth a line or two before leaving the Parque de Maria Luisa is the picturesque uniform of the guardians—the traditional dress of the Spanish game-keeper, brown with green facings and leather accessories. The tasselled leggings buttoned only at the ankle and the top particularly engaged the attention of Théophile Gautier, likewise the broad-brimmed hat with green cockade. Something about the nicety of design and emphasis of small items makes this uniform specially appropriate to the Sevillian "park police."

EL JARDIN DE MURILLO, SEVILLE

Another but very small public garden has recently been made, called the Murillo Garden. On this site the idolized Sevillian painter is supposed to have lived; certain it is that he was buried in the church of Santa Cruz, now demolished, which stood nearby. A few attractive box-bound flower-beds, good tile fountains and seats, make up the typical composition. The most notable item is the caretaker's lodge which we illustrate—a nice bit of design in the spirit of the modern revival, carried out in white stucco, and adorned by fine iron window rejas. Potted plants, the reserve supply for the garden, are set about with great prodigality. Those who enjoy looking into small details will be interested in the iron rings in the façade and again at each side of the rejas for holding flower-pots. These can also be seen on many an Andalusian balcony.

EL MUSEO PROVINCIAL, SEVILLE

A small garden carried to a high degree of finish, and beautiful in the special way that certain highly finished old paintings are beautiful, is that of the *Museo Provincial de Bellas Artes*. Until the Disestablishment of the Monasteries (1835) this was the *Convento de la Merced*, and the garden referred to is in the southern-

MARIA LUISA PARK, SEVILLE. CYPRESS ARCH
Leads to the stucco pergola

MARIA LUISA PARK. PERGOLA IN WHITE STUCCO
The insets are of green tile

THE MARIA LUISA PARK. LILY POND AND ISLAND
The curbs are made of moulded brick

A WINTER VIEW OF LILY POND AND ISLAND IN MARIA LUISA PARK

MARIA LUISA PARK. QUADRANGLE DEFINED BY A COLOURED TILE SEAT

MARIA LUISA PARK. OUTDOOR READING ROOM
Dedicated to the celebrated novelist Cervantes, and executed in coloured tiles which illustrate the history of Don Quixote

REAR DOOR AND WINDOW OPENING ON AN ABANDONED GARDEN
Seville

STUCCO DETAIL IN THE MARIA LUISA PARK

most of its two large cloisters. In design it is probably what it was when the cowled inmates laid it out, but its freshening-up is due to the modern Renaissance of garden craft in Seville. Now it is a study in blue and white tiles, yellow earth paths, and dark-green shrubs; all placed with consummate precision and admirably kept in order. As it is illustrated in colour it is hardly necessary to point out that nothing could be simpler than the scheme—wide paths of yellow earth well tamped down, narrow bisecting paths, only two feet wide, of brick tile enlivened with colour insets and edging of alternate blue and white blocks, two by eight inches; basin in blue and white checkers but reverting to green and white in the central font; yellow curbing to the yellow paths, as the juxtaposition of the blue and white blocks would have been a disturbing note. The planting is as conventional as the ceramic arrangement—low dense creepers carpet the plots, in which are set out two sizes of dwarf shrubs, one about eight inches high, the other about two feet; the contents of the alternate blue and white glazed pots which stand on the coping of the basin vary with the season, but red geraniums, carnations, and purple lilies appear most often, never two colours at the same time. Under the bright white arcade of this cloister runs a wainscot of polychrome tiles, and the walls are hung with old pictures of the Sevillian school. No detail has been overlooked, and the centre of the quadrangle is like a highly polished and beautifully laid mosaic.

NUMBER 8, GUZMAN EL BUENO, SEVILLE

As a specimen of the small city garden, and one more or less similar to many others in Seville, we illustrate that to the rear of the Osborne palace at No. 8, *Calle de Guzman el Bueno*. Portions of the house date from before the Christian reconquest, but the garden would not be anterior to the seventeenth century. It consists of two plots embraced on three sides by the house and its wings. One *motif* is square, the other oblong; between the two is a triple-arched marble screen with a delicate iron grille. For the rest the composition consists of polychrome tiles and dark-green garden plots. Flowers, except those in pots, hardly enter into the scheme. In each enclosure is a tile fountain, and against the far wall—that separating the adjoining house—a tiled bench with tall panel behind. In the arcaded gallery that surrounds the garden stand fine old pieces of Spanish furniture, and on the walls hang some excellent canvases by seventeenth-century masters, the contemporaries of Velazquez and Murillo. These help to give the garden that lived-in aspect which Sevillians may properly regard as their own special achievement.

GARDEN OF THE MARQUES DE VIANA, CORDOVA

Our remaining small flat garden is found not in Seville, but in Cordova: *Calle de las Rejas de Don Gomez*, palace of His Excellency the Marques de Viana. The curious name of the street refers to a legend wherein the three large grilles of the Viana wall figure prominently. The palace dates from the sixteenth century, but the garden appears much more ancient. It probably represents a small fraction of one of the large Moorish gardens for which Cordova was celebrated in the eleventh century—places where exotic flowers and fruits from distant India grew in profusion, where water gushed over quicksilvered glass to glisten in the sun, where rare birds of brilliant plumage, invisibly netted, darted about. Hard to visualize in the decayed city of to-day! With the exception of the great Mosque, and this sadly tampered with by Christian zeal, scarcely a vestige of Moorish architecture remains; and as for palace gardens, we are reduced to the single small example illustrated.

The Viana palace stands on the north part of the town, near the Convent of Santa Isabel. From the street one enters a spacious patio arcaded on all sides, the entrance being ingeniously arranged in a corner. At once the eye is confronted with an entirely new picture; no polychrome tiles but colour supplied instead by bright-yellow kalsomine. Stone columns of the arcade are thus painted, likewise string courses and cornices. The plants around the central fountain grow from glazed yellow pots. No other colour enters into the scheme. Under the arcade is a beautifully laid walk of black and white river stones, and the open court is of coarse white gravel. Everything here is as orderly and as polished as a ship's deck.

To reach the garden one has to pass through the palace, a Moorish way of doing things which did not in the least disturb the Spaniards. As seen in plan it is arranged on the principle of a series of open-air rooms, surrounded by lofty walls eighteen or twenty feet high, and the enclosures approximately forty feet square. The first, *de los Naranjos*, is set out with orange trees whose foliage is trained into a dense screen overhead; the black soil is carefully banked for irrigation with a not undecorative result. The second, *de las Rejas*, is devoted entirely to potted plants set about in groups on the brick pavement, and the only visible earth is that at the base of the walls where vines are planted. The third enclosure has a beautiful central group of cypresses trained in the form of a Gothic arcade and enclosing a marble fountain; off in each of the four corners is planted a huge semicircular clump of box. Here, too, there is a simple brick pavement. Access from one enclosure is by means of wooden rejas painted with blue kalsomine and the walls are covered with bougainvillea, its deep green and bright purple most effective against the white. The white façade of the house itself is set off by ultramarine blue cornice and string course, while the woodwork, such as shutters and sash, is painted green. At the level of the *piso principal* and extending almost the entire length of the garden is an imposing iron balcony; this, too, is painted green except for the *repoussé motifs* of lions and castles, which are gilded. From this balcony one gets charming views of the garden in combination with the attractive rooftops of the old town beyond.

A visit to this garden in summer, and one readily appreciates the *raison d'être* of its walls. Except when the sun is on the meridian they are always casting a welcome shadow. Lofty though they are, one never feels shut in, for besides the generous archways connecting one patio with another there are additional small openings in the form of recessed windows; also the three large ones overlooking the street and barred by the "Rejas de Don Gomez." It will be noted that this Cordova example, in contrast to those examined in Seville, is devoid of azulejos.

The smaller towns of Andalusia supply little of importance in the way of real gardens; here and there, as at Ecija, Osuna, Jerez, Cadiz, pretentious patios of considerable architectural merit and good planting may be found; but what the lesser towns chiefly yield would be small patios and garden details of a simple picturesque quality.

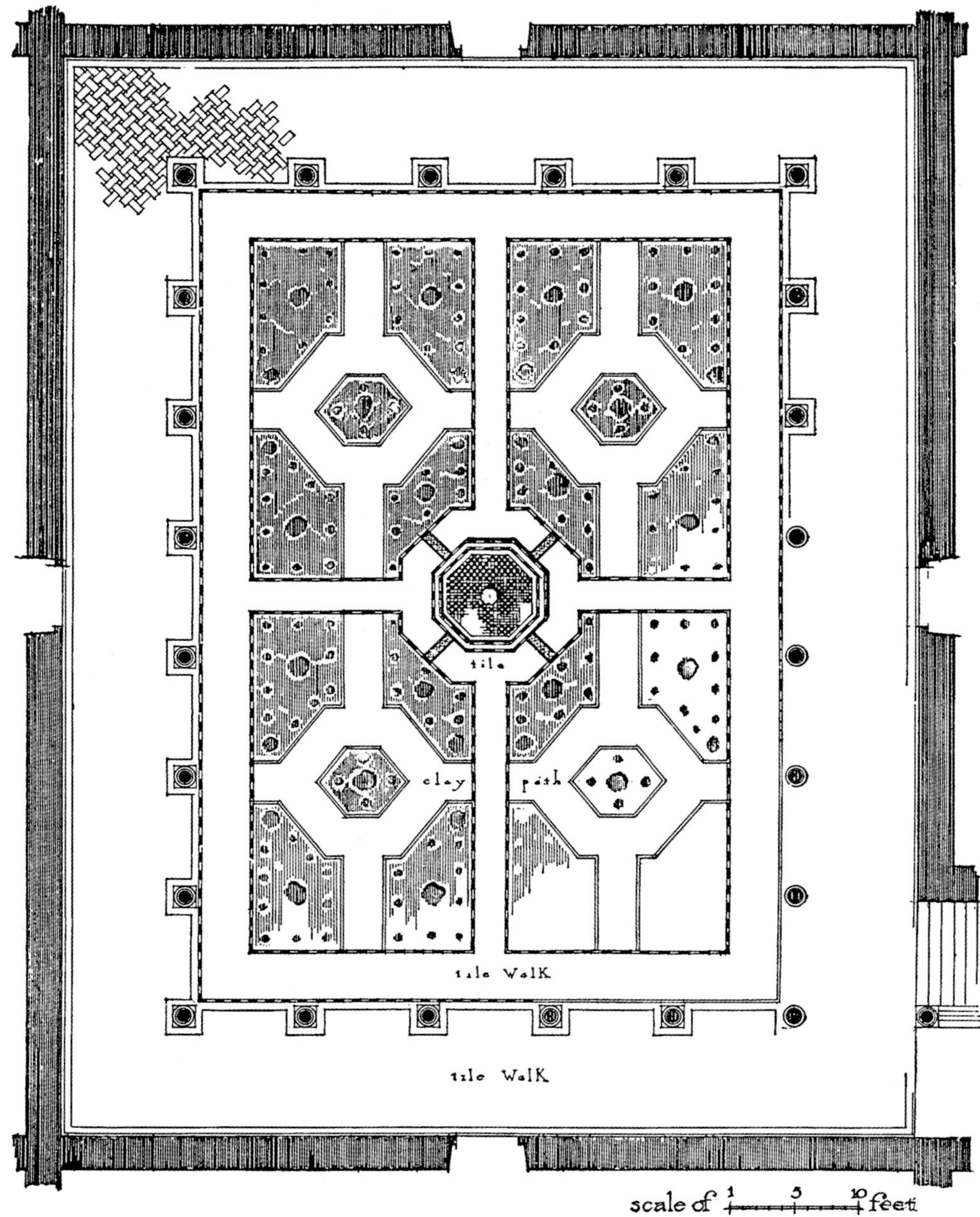

MUSEO PROVINCIAL, SEVILLE. PLAN OF THE TILED GARDEN

MUSEO PROVINCIAL, SEVILLE, DETAIL OF THE GARDEN

HOUSE IN THE CALLE DE GUZMAN EL BUENO, SEVILLE
Loggia and garden at the rear

CALLE DE GUZMAN EL BUENO
Rear garden with seat of polychrome tiles built into the white wall

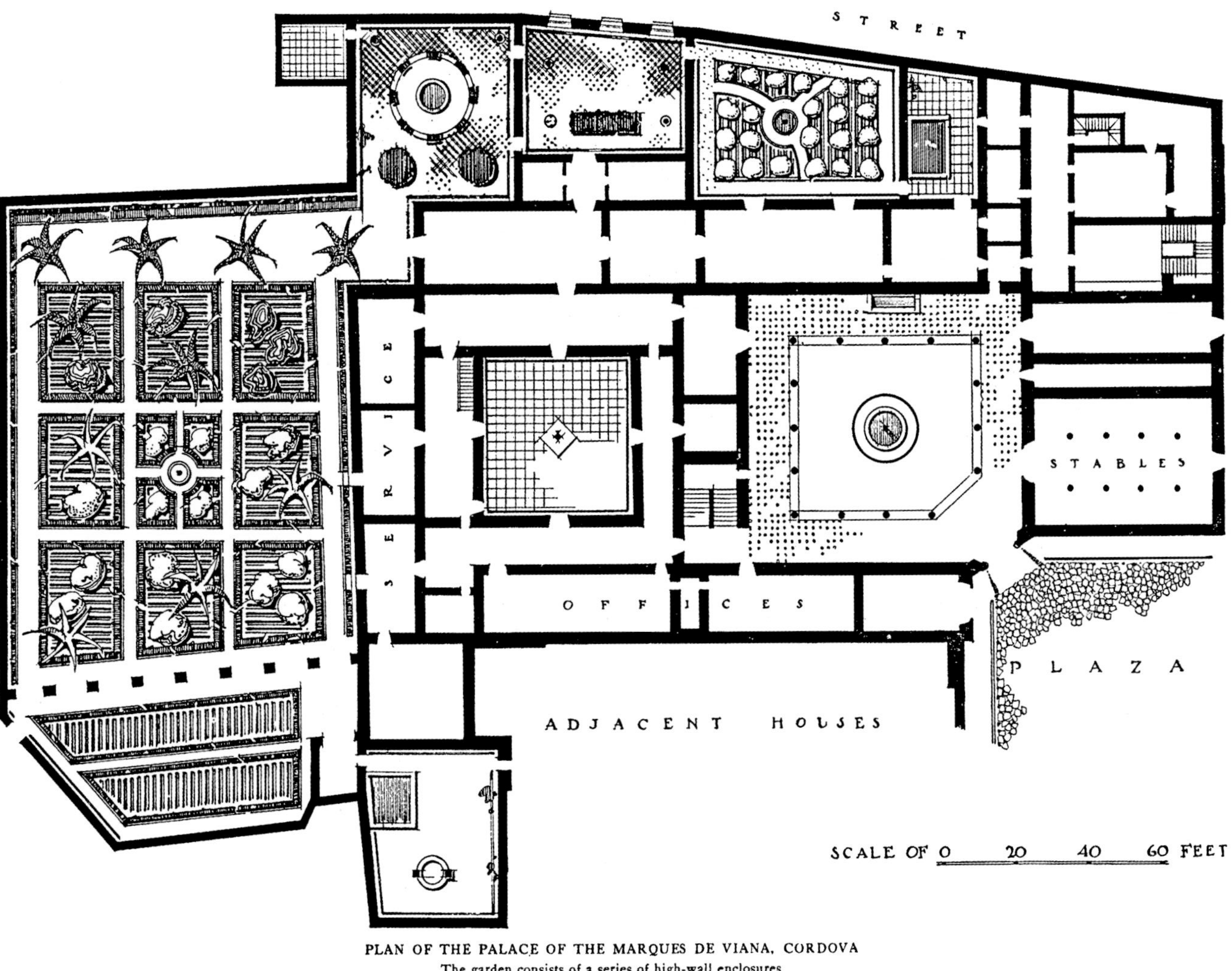

PLAN OF THE PALACE OF THE MARQUES DE VIANA, CORDOVA
The garden consists of a series of high-wall enclosures

RESIDENCE OF THE MARQUES DE VIANA. LOGGIA
Paved with river pebbles and overlooking the garden

THE VIANA GARDEN. WHITE WALLS SOFTENED BY VINES

GARDEN OF THE MARQUES DE VIANA. LOOKING FROM THE BALCONY
One of the paved enclosures whose central motif is a Gothic arcade formed by ancient cypress trees

THE VIANA GARDEN. BLUE WOODEN GATE
The vertical members are cut with the profile of a spindle

TILE PICTURE OF A PICNIC, DATED 1809, FORMERLY ENCRUSTED IN A GARDEN WALL

PART II

TYPICAL PATIOS AND GARDENS OF MAJORCA

VILLA RUBERT, BAY OF PALMA
An exedra in the garden overlooking the city

PART II

TYPICAL PATIOS AND GARDENS OF MAJORCA

IN COMMON with Andalusia, the Balearic Islands have the blue Mediterranean for a background and a North African climate. Mediterranean architecture from Gibraltar to Suez has a certain similarity derived from sun-crisped walls of varying colour, flat roofs, gaily painted accessories, and vine-covered walks. Majorca (Spanish, *Mallorca*) has all this and, besides, more serious elements in plenty, for the palaces of Palma, the capital, are an interesting combination of Catalan Gothic and Genoese Renaissance.

The natural beauty of the island—lofty mountains to the west, a great plain to the east, the sea visible from every point; weirdly twisted olive trees that boast a thousand years, wide-spreading carobs, pines; almond trees that convert the whole island into a cloud of blossoms in January, and orange and lemon trees that live in close intimacy with the house itself—all this form and colour make set planting seem superfluous. Majorcan gardens have their attraction but it is not that of studied formal planting.

A glance at the patios in Palma before going farther afield. We have said that the palaces reflect Catalan and Genoese influence. The old half-Moorish, half-Gothic city was nearly destroyed by fire in the fifteenth century. As it had even from Moorish days been in close commercial relations with Genoa in particular and

Italy in general, it was natural that the nobles in rebuilding their palaces should turn to a land that excelled in the then modern architecture. The sombre façades are imposing though they generally face on a street no wider than six or eight feet—immense arched portal, beautifully framed Renaissance windows, and an open gallery under the far-projecting eaves. These last are reminiscent of Aragon and Catalonia. On turning into the patio, however, we find a sturdy sort of Renaissance that harks back to Genoa and Florence but without much Genoese and Florentine refinement. Gothic patios too can be found, saved from the flames or subsequently rebuilt in the old tradition.

Though varied in treatment, Palma patios are alike in their ample proportions, all the more noticeable on turning in from the narrow street. Unlike the Andalusian feature, it is not gay and colourful ; not an outdoor room to be lived in. Of solid masonry, it is essentially a practical court leading to the stairs and used by both family and servants. Architecturally it is more developed than the Andalusian patio. Its staircase always arouses admiration ; not enclosed but rising from the open in a single run, it then divides into two returning flights which lead to the loggia-like gallery of the main floor. In patios that cling to the Gothic tradition the stair is a long single run against one side and supported on an arch so flat that one wonders how the stones stay in place. All these stairways have a rail of beaten iron cut to the silhouette of a stone baluster and topped off at the landings with brass, a very individual arrangement not seen on the mainland. The bays around the open patio are vaulted but in a few of the older palaces the vestibule leading from the street has a Moorish painted wooden ceiling. Vines or potted plants rarely relieve the mediæval stoniness.

The Majorcan garden is not found in connexion with the city palace but is part of the *posesiòn*, or tract which Don Jaime gave to each of the chieftains who brought troops to help in the conquest of the island. A more common name for these country places is *son*. In many cases the *son* is still held by descendants of the warrior on whom it was bestowed in the thirteenth century. The house itself is usually simple, even when reformed in the seventeenth century, at which time the island, in contrast to the rest of Spain, was enjoying its usual prosperity.

According to ancient custom the *son* is managed by the *amo*, or lessee-farmer, and his wife, the *madona* ; to it the owner resorts occasionally for short stays. Under one roof are his quarters, those for the amo, the chapel, and various storehouses, olive presses, and so forth, making a picturesque stucco pile crowned by tiled roofs. The patio, called in Mallorquin the *clasta*, is either shaded by a giant grape-vine or a spreading tree in the centre, and is often overlooked by a gallery on one side. Although the stair is generally enclosed like the claustral type of Andalusia, a subsidiary flight often rises from one corner to a mezzanine, and its iron balustrade and lean-to wooden hood add interest to the *clasta* composition; so likewise does the chapel entrance with its niched saint above. The well, common to all patios in all parts of Spain, has an iron crane and stone kerb on which stands the classic copper *cântaro*.

In this brief space we can mention only a few such possessions: on the road to Soller we find first *Raxa*, remodelled in the late eighteenth century by Majorca's famous patron of art, Cardinal Despuig; a few kilometers farther on the left, *S'Auqueria* (la Alqueria, or manor); while on the right stands *Alfabia*. On the road to Bañalbufar is *La Granja* (the grange) and quite near to Palma, *Son Berga* and *Sarriá*. Only a half-hour's walk from the Son Rapiña tram are *Son Vida* and *La Cigale*; *Son Veri* lies on the great highroad to Inca, while *El Salt* (the cascade) *de Son Forteza* is romantically situated up in the western mountain chain beyond Puigpuñent. A beautiful cloister garden and terrace is that of the Señora de Bonsoms, who lives in the former Carthusian Monastery of Valdemosa; and lastly, almost within the limits of Palma itself, is the lovely old seaside garden, *El Jardin Rubert*, which has made effective use of the Gothic capitals and saints from a ruined convent that stood near the site.

Raxa, to which Cardinal Despuig retired after a long residence in Rome and whither he brought many shiploads of antique art treasures, was already an old estate. Before passing to the illustrious Despuig family (through intermarriage) in the early seventeenth century, it had

CLOISTER OF THE CONVENTO DE SAN FRANCISCO, PALMA
A fourteenth-century inclosure with informal planting

PATIO OF THE ALMUDAINA OR MOORISH ROYAL PALACE, PALMA
Remodeled after the Christian Conquest

PATIO OF THE CASA LASTRE, PALMA
In the smaller houses mediaeval tradition never completely disappeared

PATIO OF THE VIVOT PALACE, PALMA. SEVENTEENTH CENTURY
Compared with the narrow streets the patios are expansive

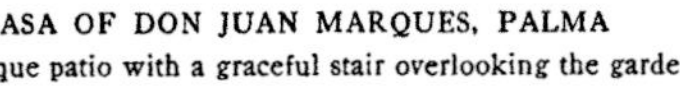

CASA OF DON JUAN MARQUES, PALMA
A Baroque patio with a graceful stair overlooking the garden

PATIO OF THE VERÍ PALACE, PALMA. SIXTEENTH CENTURY
Service entrance, the great stair being in the foremost bay

belonged for some two hundred years or more to the Sa-Fortezas, whose great city palace is the present Post Office; and to judge by its Arab name, Raxa had previously been the estate of a Moor of high degree. The last inheritor, the now aged Conde de Montenegro, being impoverished, sold it and the contents of its famous library and museum; only a few statues and lapidary inscriptions remain.

The Raxa garden, reminiscent of the Italian, is to-day very charming in its moss-covered dilapidation. The site was chosen for its natural supply of water, the first consideration on an island where droughts are frequent. Better to control the supply a large lake was made, which may date, like all the reservoirs on the island, from Moorish days. The garden belongs to the hillside type, for it nestles in the *falda* (lap) of the Valdemosa mountains; but unlike the Andalusian examples in the same class no decorative devices were resorted to for bringing the water down to the various levels; instead, there is an inconspicuous little canal, stone-lined, behind the parapet. There is only one fountain to speak of — that of the parterre in front of the house; but many have been sold from the place. The great feature is the monumental stone stairway which leads from the *piso principal* of the house, one story higher than the patio level, up to the reservoir. Flanked with stepped parterres planted with great masses of purple iris (which, by the way, grows in amazing profusion in Majorca), and these overhung by orange trees and lofty dark pines, the colour effect is very beautiful and compensates for the mediocrity of the statuary.

It is interesting to note that the balustrade of the Raxa loggia and terraces, always more Italian than Spanish, is here provided with hollow terra-cotta balusters. Whether these particular examples set the fashion or not is hard to say, but similar ones are found on every estate on this side of the island. From the uppermost terrace a good bird's-eye view of the house is obtained—a simple quadrangle in plan, enclosing a spacious patio, and, rising from the interesting jumble of tiled roofs, a little belfry for calling the hands to meals and to mass. Below and to the south of the house is a small sunken garden with formal beds lined with box, and interesting steps and armorial portal leading up to the main road.

Alfabia (another Moorish name) is even more interesting in its way. The house is approached by a long avenue of sycamores with beautiful whitish trunks. The windowless Baroque façade is merely a factitious front deliberately set up only a few feet in advance of the original Gothic façade. The patio has the usual picturesque accessories—well, chapel, olive presses, and cavernous storeroom for almonds. Off to the left, before entering the patio, and reached by another avenue of sycamores, lies the garden, its portal flanked on one side by a Baroque dove-cote and on the other by a stone-vaulted reservoir. This pool probably dates from Moorish days, for Alfabia was once the country seat of the Moorish governor.

The main walk of the garden is in the form of a long trellis sloping down to the orange groves that extend back of the house; on the one side indiscriminate planting of flowers, on the other formal beds. Pebbles were used for the patterned pavement of the walk; besides the vines that shade it, it is further cooled by side sprays of water from lead jets in the parapet wall, following Moorish tradition. At the end of the walk is a fountain of no artistic merit but supplied with metal attachments that throw the water into myriad forms. A very serious and very small boy can be persuaded for very small compensation to juggle golden oranges in the slender jet by the hour, for the lucky visitor who has time to linger.

Another *son* illustrated, *Sa Forteza*, is beyond the town of Puigpuñent in a remote valley. To reach it one might take the road between Valdemosa and Esporlas and include the magnificent *Son Canet*. The Sa Forteza place is alluded to locally as *El Salt*, in reference to the cascade that leaps from the lofty crags behind the house. Approaching from the road, one sees a succession of broad terraces leading up to the house like a stupendous flight of steps. They are planted with close-clipped orange trees that appear as diminutive as the little tufts in primitive pictures. Once on top and passing through the patio one sees that the uppermost level has been reserved for a beautiful green garden whose only bloom is the purple iris. Hedges of box are arranged in simple geometric patterns, each dominated by a clipped palm or stiff pine. One feels that anything more would be wrong; the landscape is too beautifully wild to need it. Especially suitable also to the picture is the simple rectangular manor made imposing by spreading bastions and without any other adornment than its many plain iron balconies. A liberal use of ochre, sea-green, and washed-out pink in the walls is not only a harmonious note, but prevents the house from seeming like a white patch on the landscape.

At Establiments, seven kilometers from Palma on the Esporlas route, is *Son Berga*. The name "establishments" refers to a parcelling up of the vast old possession of *Son Gual* into some five or six estates in the early eighteenth century, the new owners building themselves houses of the classic island type. Thus Son Berga and Sarriá came into existence. The Berga has a fine site—an extensive plateau high above the road and commanding the whole Bay of Palma in front and the mountain range to the north and west. A stately main façade is featured by a triple-arched loggia set above a mediæval-looking vaulted passage connecting patio and formal garden. The garden of close-clipped hedges, bright clay paths, and several creditable fountains, is quite free of any high growth that would interrupt the sweep of city and sea. At the back, in contrast, is an English garden of masses of flowers, winding paths, the great drive that terminates at the patio entrance, and many tall shade trees. On a little eminence in this part of the grounds is preserved one of the old windmills with which the Gual tract was dotted, with its niched Virgin above the

THE PATIO AND LOGGIA OVERLOOKING THE GARDEN AT LA GRANJA
Its seventeenth-century builders were thoroughly conversant with Florentine architecture

THE PATIO AT RAXA, THE DESPUIG COUNTRY SEAT
An old villa remodeled in the late eighteenth century

RAXA, THE ESTATE OF CARDINAL DESPUIG, MAJORCA. THE ESTANQUE OR RESERVOIR
Its foundations are of Moorish origin

THE GARDEN STAIR AT RAXA
On each side of the parapets are little canals for watering the terraces

THE GARDENS AT RAXA. THE MONUMENTAL STAIR LEADING TO THE RESERVOIR
Purple iris, orange trees, and pines are on each side

ALFABIA, AN ESTATE ON THE ROAD TO SOLLER, MAJORCA
The villa is approached by a long avenue of sycamores

THE APPROACH TO ALFABIA SEEN FROM WITHIN THE PATIO
Though the façade is Baroque the nucleus of the house dates from the fifteenth century

THE GARDEN PERGOLA AT ALFABIA LEADING TO THE ORANGE GROVES
In summer this is freshened by jets of water at the sides

THE GARDEN GATE AT ALFABIA
Its charm does not depend upon a profound knowledge of architecture

SON SA FORTEZA IN THE MOUNTAINS OF PUIGPUÑENT MAJORCA
The villa crowns a succession of imposing orange-clad terraces

THE UPPER TERRACE OF SON SA FORTEZA
The planting is kept subordinate to nature

SON BERGA, AN EIGHTEENTH-CENTURY VILLA AT ESTABLIMENTS, MAJORCA

A broad terrace of formal planting in front of the house commands the Bay of Palma

THE PATIO OF SON BERGA AND THE FACADE OF THE ORIGINAL FIFTEENTH CENTURY FARM-HOUSE

GARDENS OF THE VILLA RUBERT, PALMA

From cleverly devised sunken pockets provided with stone benches and tables one may view the Mediterranean regardless of summer heat

GARDENS OF THE VILLA RUBERT, PALMA
Mediterranean gardeners are but little interested in classic accessories

THE TOMATO TERRACES AT BAÑULBUFAR, MAJORCA
A most extraordinary Mediterranean composition achieved by centuries of patient toil

portal. It now serves as a dove-cote. Sloping northwards from the house and its two gardens is the *huerta* or farm. Son Berga harbors a number of interesting antiquities that were found on the island.

Hardly to be classed as gardens, yet of great interest, are the terraces of Bañalbufar, a picturesque town on the west coast. Man by centuries of toil has rendered fertile the once rocky slopes to the sea, terracing them in such perfect conformity to the natural topography that it all appears to have been so from the beginning. Seen from the high-perched coast drive coming from Esporlas, the whole stretch looks like a big relief map scored with the engineer's contour lines. Warmed by the reflected heat of the Mediterranean which laps the foot of the hills, and gay with the colour of varied flowers and fruits (tomatoes being one of the chief products), these terraces provide a very considerable annual income to their owners.

Altogether a most alluring spot is this little-known island of Mallorca. The garden-lover could ask for nothing more poetic than its old-time, never too scientifically laid-out gardens; yet we present them well aware that neither pen nor camera has done full justice to their charm.

INDEX

INDEX